Rick Steves®

POCKET

PARIS

Rick Steves, Steve Smith & Gene Openshaw

Contents

Introduction

Paris—the City of Light—has been a beacon of culture for centuries. As a world capital of art, fashion, food, literature, and ideas, it stands as a symbol of all the fine things human civilization can offer. Come prepared to celebrate this, rather than judge our cultural differences, and you'll capture the romance and joie de vivre that Paris exudes.

Paris offers sweeping boulevards, chatty crêpe stands, chic boutiques, and world-class art galleries. Sip decaf with deconstructionists at a sidewalk café, then step into an Impressionist painting in a tree-lined park. Climb Notre-Dame and rub shoulders with a gargoyle. Cruise the Seine, zip up the Eiffel Tower, and saunter down Avenue des Champs-Elysées. Master the Louvre and Orsay museums. Save some after-dark energy for one of the world's most romantic cities.

Introduction

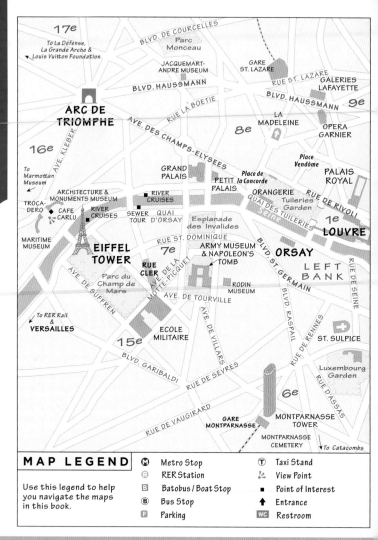

17e

To La Défense,
La Grande Arche &
Louis Vuitton Foundation

BLVD. DE COURCELLES

Parc
Monceau

JACQUEMART-
ANDRE MUSEUM

GARE
ST. LAZARE

RUE ST. LAZARE

GALERIES
LAFAYETTE

BLVD. HAUSSMANN

BLVD. HAUSSMANN

9e

ARC DE
TRIOMPHE

RUE LA BOETIE

LA
MADELEINE

OPERA
GARNIER

16e

AVE. DES CHAMPS-ELYSEES

8e

AVE. KLEBER

To
Marmottan
Museum

GRAND
PALAIS

PETIT
PALAIS

Place de
la Concorde

Place
Vendôme

PALAIS
ROYAL

ARCHITECTURE &
MONUMENTS MUSEUM

RIVER
CRUISES

ORANGERIE

RUE DE RIVOLI

TROCA-
DERO

CAFE
CARLU

RIVER
CRUISES

SEWER
TOUR

QUAI
D'ORSAY

Esplanade
des Invalides

Tuileries
Garden

QUAI DES TUILERIES

Seine

1e

LOUVRE

MARITIME
MUSEUM

EIFFEL
TOWER

RUE ST. DOMINIQUE

7e

ARMY MUSEUM
& NAPOLEON'S
TOMB

ORSAY

LEFT
BANK

RUE CLER

RUE DE LA
MOTTE-PICQUET

BLVD. ST. GERMAIN

RUE DE SEINE

Parc du
Champ de
Mars

RODIN
MUSEUM

AVE. DE TOURVILLE

BLVD. RASPAIL

AVE. DE SUFFREN

To RER Rail
&
VERSAILLES

ECOLE
MILITAIRE

AVE. DE VILLARS

ST. SULPICE

15e

RUE DE RENNES

BLVD. GARIBALDI

RUE DE SEVRES

Luxembourg
Garden

RUE D'ASSAS

6e

RUE DE VAUGIRARD

GARE
MONTPARNASSE

MONTPARNASSE
TOWER

MONTPARNASSE
CEMETERY

To Catacombs

MAP LEGEND

Use this legend to help
you navigate the maps
in this book.

Ⓜ Metro Stop
Ⓡ RER Station
Ⓑ Batobus / Boat Stop
Ⓑ Bus Stop
Ⓟ Parking

Ⓣ Taxi Stand
⅄ View Point
■ Point of Interest
✦ Entrance
WC Restroom

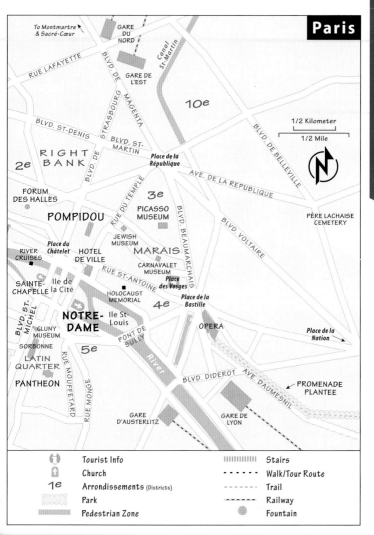

Paris

To Montmartre & Sacré-Cœur

GARE DU NORD

GARE DE L'EST

Canal St-Martin

RUE LAFAYETTE

BLVD. DE MAGENTA

BLVD. DE STRASBOURG

10e

1/2 Kilometer

1/2 Mile

BLVD. ST-DENIS

BLVD. ST-MARTIN

BLVD. DE BELLEVILLE

2e

RIGHT BANK

Place de la République

AVE. DE LA REPUBLIQUE

N

FORUM DES HALLES

3e

PICASSO MUSEUM

RUE DU TEMPLE

BLVD. BEAUMARCHAIS

PÈRE LACHAISE CEMETERY

POMPIDOU

BLVD. VOLTAIRE

JEWISH MUSEUM

Place du Châtelet

RIVER CRUISES

HOTEL DE VILLE

MARAIS

CARNAVALET MUSEUM

SAINTE-CHAPELLE

Ile de la Cité

RUE ST-ANTOINE

Place des Vosges

BLVD. ST-MICHEL

CLUNY MUSEUM

NOTRE-DAME

HOLOCAUST MEMORIAL

4e

Place de la Bastille

Ile St-Louis

OPERA

Place de la Nation

SORBONNE

PONT DE SULLY

River

LATIN QUARTER

5e

RUE MONGE

RUE MOUFFETARD

PANTHEON

BLVD. DIDEROT

AVE DAUMESNIL

PROMENADE PLANTEE

GARE D'AUSTERLITZ

GARE DE LYON

Symbol	Meaning	Symbol	Meaning
🛈	Tourist Info	|||||||	Stairs
⛪	Church	- - - - -	Walk/Tour Route
1e	Arrondissements (Districts)	- - - - - -	Trail
🟫	Park	- - - - - -	Railway
▦	Pedestrian Zone	●	Fountain

About This Book

With this book, I've selected only the best of Paris—admittedly, a tough call. The core of the book is six self-guided walks and tours that zero in on Paris' greatest sights and neighborhoods. The Historic Paris Walk takes you through the heart of the city—soaring Notre-Dame, the bustling Latin Quarter, and the stained-glass wonder of Sainte-Chapelle. You'll see all the essentials of the vast Louvre and Orsay museums, while still leaving time for browsing. Ascend the 1,000-foot Eiffel Tower at sunset and watch the City of Light up. Stroll Rue Cler's friendly (and odiferous) shops, and take a side-trip to Versailles for chandeliered palaces and manicured gardens.

The rest of the book is a traveler's tool kit. You'll find plenty more about Paris' attractions, from shopping to nightlife to less touristy sights. And there are helpful hints on saving money, avoiding crowds, getting around on the Métro, finding a great meal, and much more.

If you'd like more information than this Pocket Guide offers, I've sprinkled the book liberally with web references. For general travel tips—as well as updates for this book—see www.ricksteves.com.

Key to This Book

Sights are rated:

    ▲▲▲ **Don't miss**
      ▲▲ **Try hard to see**
        ▲ **Worthwhile if you can make it**
No rating **Worth knowing about**

Tourist information offices are abbreviated as **TI**, bathrooms are **WC**s, and Métro stops are **Mo**.

Like Europe, this book uses the **24-hour clock**. It's the same through 12:00 noon, then keeps going: 13:00 (1:00 p.m.), 14:00 (2:00 p.m), and so on.

For opening times, if a sight is listed as "May-Oct daily 9:00-18:00," it's open from 9 a.m. until 6 p.m. from the first day of May until the last day of October.

Paris by Neighborhood

Central Paris (population 2.3 million) is circled by a ring road, and split in half by the Seine River, which runs east-west. If you were on a boat floating downstream, the Right Bank would be on your right, and the Left Bank on your left. The bull's-eye on your map is Notre-Dame, on an island in the middle of the Seine and ground zero in Paris.

Twenty arrondissements (administrative districts) spiral out from the center, like an escargot shell. If your hotel's zip code is 75007, you know (from the last two digits) that it's in the 7th arrondissement. The city is peppered with Métro stops, and most Parisians locate addresses by the closest stop. So in Parisian jargon, the Eiffel Tower is on *la Rive Gauche* (the Left Bank) in the *7ème* (7th arrondissement), zip code 75007, Mo: Trocadéro (the nearest Métro stop).

Think of Paris as a series of neighborhoods, cradling major landmarks.

Historic Core: Paris got its start around Notre-Dame, on the Ile de la

Introduction

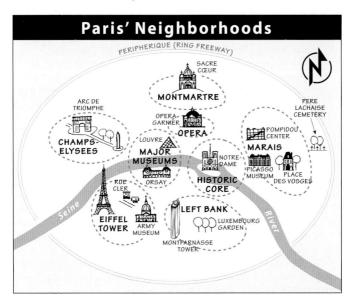

Paris' Neighborhoods

PERIPHERIQUE (RING FREEWAY)

SACRE CŒUR

MONTMARTRE

ARC DE TRIOMPHE

PERE LACHAISE CEMETERY

OPERA-GARNIER

OPERA

CHAMPS-ELYSEES

LOUVRE

MAJOR MUSEUMS

POMPIDOU CENTER

MARAIS

NOTRE-DAME

PICASSO MUSEUM

PLACE DES VOSGES

RUE CLER

ORSAY

HISTORIC CORE

Seine

EIFFEL TOWER

ARMY MUSEUM

LEFT BANK

LUXEMBOURG GARDEN

River

MONTPARNASSE TOWER

Daily Reminder

Sunday: Many sights are free on the first Sunday of the month, including the Orsay, Cluny, Pompidou, and Picasso museums. Several sights are free on the first Sunday during winter, including the Louvre, Rodin Museum, and Arc de Triomphe (Oct-March), and all the sights at Versailles (Nov-March). These free days at popular sights attract hordes of visitors. Versailles is more crowded than usual on Sunday, and when the garden's fountains run (April-Oct).

Look for organ concerts at St. Sulpice and other churches. The American Church often has free classical piano concerts June-Sept at 17:00 (near the Eiffel Tower, 65 Quai d'Orsay, acparis.org). Luxembourg Garden has puppet shows.

Most of Paris' stores are closed on Sunday, but shoppers will find relief along the Champs-Elysées (traffic-free on first Sun of the month), at flea markets, and in the Marais neighborhood. Many recommended restaurants in the Rue Cler neighborhood are closed for dinner.

Monday: These sights are closed today: Orsay, Rodin, Marmottan, Picasso, Catacombs, Petit Palais, Victor Hugo's House, Archaeological Crypt, Jewish Art and History Museum, Deportation Memorial, and Versailles (but the gardens are open). The Louvre is far more crowded because of these closings. Off-season, the Army Museum is closed the first Monday of the month, but Napoleon's Tomb stays open.

Market streets such as Rue Cler and Rue Mouffetard are dead today.

Cité ("Island of the City"). There you'll find Paris' oldest sights, from Roman ruins to the medieval Sainte-Chapelle church.

Major Museums Neighborhood: To the west, the Louvre, Orsay, and Orangerie museums cluster around the fringes of the Tuileries Garden

Champs-Elysées: The greatest 19th-century boulevard runs northwest from Place de la Concorde to the Arc de Triomphe.

Eiffel Tower Neighborhood: In the tower's shadow lies colorful Rue Cler, with its village-like market, the Army Museum and Napoleon's Tomb, and the Rodin Museum.

Opéra Neighborhood: Along with elegant sights such as the Opéra

Tuesday: Many sights are closed today, including the Louvre, Orangerie, Cluny, and Pompidou museums. The Orsay and Versailles are crazy busy. The gardens at Versailles have music and/or fountain displays in summer (check hours). Napoleon's Tomb is open until 21:00 (April-Sept).

Wednesday: All sights are open, and some have late hours, including the Louvre (until 21:45, last entry 21:00). The weekly *L'officiel des Spectacles* magazine comes out today. Most schools are closed, so kids' sights are busy, and puppet shows play in Luxembourg Garden.

Thursday: All sights are open except the Sewer Tour. Some sights are open late, including the Orsay (until 21:45, last entry 21:00) and Marmottan (21:00). Some department stores are open late.

Friday: All sights are open except the Sewer Tour. The Louvre is open until 21:45 (last entry 21:00) and Notre-Dame's tower until 23:00 (July-Aug). Afternoon trains and roads leaving Paris are crowded. Restaurants are busy—it's smart to book ahead.

Saturday: All sights are open except the Holocaust Memorial. The fountains run at Versailles April-Oct (nice but very crowded). Notre-Dame's tower is open until 23:00 (July-Aug). Department stores are jammed and restaurants are packed—reserve ahead. In summer, puppet shows are held at Luxembourg Garden.

Garnier, the neighborhood also offers high-end shopping.

Left Bank: Between the river and the Luxembourg Garden, the Left Bank is known for Paris' intellectual, artistic, and café life. It's also one of Paris' best boutique shopping areas.

Marais: Stretching eastward along Rue de Rivoli/Rue St. Antoine to Place Bastille, this neighborhood is the upwardly mobile Paris of today—with trendy restaurants, shops, nightlife, and artistic sights such as the Pompidou Center and Picasso Museum.

Montmartre: This hill, topped by the bulbous white domes of Sacré-Cœur, hovers on the northern fringes of your Paris map. The neighborhood

Paris at a Glance

▲▲▲ **Notre-Dame Cathedral** Paris' most beloved church, with towers and gargoyles. **Hours:** Cathedral—Mon-Sat 7:45-18:45, Sun 7:15-19:15; Tower—daily April-Sept 10:00-18:30, Fri-Sat until 23:00 in July-Aug, Oct-March 10:00-17:30. See page 17.

▲▲▲ **Sainte-Chapelle** Gothic cathedral with peerless stained glass. **Hours:** Daily April-Sept 9:00-19:00, Oct-March until 17:00. See page 33.

▲▲▲ **Louvre** Europe's oldest and greatest museum, starring *Mona Lisa* and *Venus de Milo*. **Hours:** Wed-Mon 9:00-18:00, Wed and Fri until 21:45, closed Tue. See page 43.

▲▲▲ **Orsay Museum** Nineteenth-century art, including Europe's greatest Impressionist collection. **Hours:** Tue-Sun 9:30-18:00, Thu until 21:45, closed Mon. See page 69.

▲▲▲ **Eiffel Tower** Paris' soaring exclamation point. **Hours:** Daily mid-June-Aug 9:00-24:45, Sept-mid-June 9:30-23:45. See page 99.

▲▲▲ **Champs-Elysées** Paris' grand boulevard. **Hours:** Always open. See page 159.

▲▲▲ **Versailles** The ultimate royal palace (Château), with a Hall of Mirrors, vast gardens, a grand canal, plus a queen's playground. **Hours:** Château April-Oct Tue-Sun 8:30-19:00, Nov-March 9:00-17:30; Trianon/Domaine de Marie-Antoinette April-Oct Tue-Sun 12:00-18:30, Nov-March until 17:30; gardens generally April-Oct daily 8:00-20:30, Nov-March until 18:00; entire complex closed Mon year-round except the Gardens. See page 121.

▲▲▲ **Picasso Museum** World's largest collection of Picasso's works. **Hours:** Tue-Fri 10:30-18:00 Sat-Sun 9:30-18:00, closed Mon. See page 166.

▲▲ **Orangerie Museum** Monet's water lilies and Modernist classics in a lovely setting. **Hours:** Wed-Mon 9:00-18:00, closed Tue. See page 149.

▲▲ **Rue Cler** Ultimate Parisian market street. **Hours:** Stores open Tue-Sat 8:30-13:00 & 15:00-19:30, Sun 8:30-12:00, dead on Mon. See page 111.

▲▲ **Army Museum and Napoleon's Tomb** The emperor's imposing tomb, flanked by museums of France's wars. **Hours:** Daily 10:00-18:00, Nov-March until 17:00; tomb also open July-Aug until 19:00 and

April-Sept Tue until 21:00; museum (except for tomb) closed first Mon of month Oct-June; Charles de Gaulle exhibit closed Mon year-round. See page 152.

▲▲ **Rodin Museum** Works by the greatest sculptor since Michelangelo, with many statues in a peaceful garden. **Hours:** Tue-Sun 10:00-17:45, closed Mon. See page 153.

▲▲ **Marmottan Museum** Art museum focusing on Monet. **Hours:** Tue-Sun 10:00-18:00, Thu until 21:00, closed Mon. See page 154.

▲▲ **Cluny Museum** Medieval art with unicorn tapestries. **Hours:** Wed-Mon 9:15-17:45, closed Tue. See page 156.

▲▲ **Arc de Triomphe** Triumphal arch marking start of Champs-Elysées. **Hours:** Interior daily 10:00-23:00, Oct-March until 22:30. See page 161.

▲▲ **Opéra Garnier** Grand belle époque theater with a modern ceiling by Chagall. **Hours:** Generally daily 10:00-16:30, mid-July-Aug until 18:00. See page 162.

▲▲ **Jacquemart-André Museum** Art-strewn mansion. **Hours:** Daily 10:00-18:00, Mon until 20:30 during special exhibits. See page 163.

▲▲ **Pompidou Center** Modern art in colorful building with city views. **Hours:** Permanent collection open Wed-Mon 11:00-21:00, closed Tue. See page 168.

▲▲ **Sacré-Cœur and Montmartre** White basilica atop Montmartre with spectacular views. **Hours:** Daily 6:00-22:30; dome climb daily May-Sept 9:30-19:00, Oct-April until 17:00. See page 169.

▲ **Panthéon** Neoclassical monument and burial place of the famous. **Hours:** Daily 10:00-18:30, Oct-March until 18:00. See page 158.

▲ **Jewish Art and History Museum** History of Judaism in Europe. **Hours:** Tue-Fri 11:00-18:00, Sat-Sun 10:00-18:00, open later during special exhibits, closed Mon year-round. See page 167.

▲ **Père Lachaise Cemetery** Final home of Paris' illustrious dead. **Hours:** Mon-Fri 8:00-18:00, Sat 8:30-18:00, Sun 9:00-18:00, until 17:30 in winter. See page 168.

still retains some of the untamed rural charm that once drew Impressionist painters and turn-of-the-century bohemians.

Planning Your Time

The following day-plans give an idea of how much an organized, motivated, and caffeinated person can see. Trying to do too much would drive you in-Seine, so leave a few things for your next visit to Paris. Paris is a great one-week getaway. If you have less than a week, start with the Day 1 plan—the most important sights—and add on from there.

Day 1: Follow this book's Historic Paris Walk. In the afternoon, tour the Louvre. Then enjoy the Trocadéro scene and a twilight ride up the Eiffel Tower.

Day 2: Stroll the Champs-Elysées from the Arc de Triomphe to the Tuileries Garden. Tour the Orsay Museum. In the evening, take a nighttime tour by cruise boat, taxi/Uber, bus, or retro-chic Deux Chevaux car.

Day 3: Catch the RER suburban train by 7:45 to arrive early at Versailles. Tour the palace's interior. Then either tour the gardens or return to Paris for more sightseeing.

Day 4: Visit Montmartre and the Sacré-Cœur Basilica. Have lunch on Montmartre. Continue your Impressionist theme by touring the Orangerie. Enjoy dinner on Ile St. Louis, then a floodlit walk by Notre-Dame.

Day 5: Concentrate on the morning market in the Rue Cler neighborhood, then afternoon sightseeing at the Rodin Museum and the Army Museum and Napoleon's Tomb.

Day 6: Ride scenic bus #69 to the Marais and tour this neighborhood, including the Pompidou Center. In the afternoon, visit the Opéra Garnier, and end your day with rooftop views from the Galeries Lafayette or Printemps department stores. Or ride the Paris Ferris Wheel, if it's spinning.

Day 7: See more in Paris (Left Bank shopping stroll, Père Lachaise Cemetery, Marmottan or Jacquemart-André museum), or take a day-trip to Chartres or Giverny.

These are busy day-plans, so be sure to schedule in slack time for picnics, laundry, people-watching, leisurely dinners, shopping, and re-charging your touristic batteries. Slow down and be open to unexpected experiences and the courtesy of Parisians.

Quick Tips: Here are a few quick sightseeing tips to get you start-ed—for more on these topics and other ideas, ✪ see page 207. Consider the handy Paris Museum Pass, which covers admission to most sights and lets you skip ticket-buying lines. Reservations are recommended for the Eiffel Tower (book early). Since opening hours are variable, get the latest information from museum websites, at www.parisinfo.com, or from local publications when you arrive. Take advantage of my free 🎧 Paris audio tours, covering many of this book's sights.

And finally, remember that—although Paris' sights can be crowded and stressful—the city itself is all about gentility and grace, so...be flexible.

I hope you have a great trip! Traveling like a temporary local, you'll get the absolute most out of every mile, minute, and euro. As you visit places I know and love, I'm happy you'll be meeting my favorite Parisians.

Bon voyage!

Historic Paris Walk

Ile de la Cité and the Latin Quarter

Paris has been the cultural capital of Europe for centuries. We'll start where it did, on Ile de la Cité, with a foray onto the Left Bank, on a walk that laces together 80 generations of history—from Celtic fishing village to Roman city, bustling medieval capital, birthplace of the Revolution, bohemian haunt of the 1920s café scene, and the working world of modern Paris. Along the way, we'll step into two of Paris' greatest sights: Notre-Dame and Sainte-Chapelle.

    Allow a good four hours for this three-mile walk, including time inside the sights. Allow a little more time to pause for lunch or a café crème, to browse for antique books, or to watch the lazy flow of the timeless Seine.

ORIENTATION

Paris Museum Pass: Several sights on this walk that charge admission are covered by the time- and money-saving Museum Pass (✪ see page 208 for details). On Ile de la Cité, you can buy a pass at the tourist-friendly *tabac*/souvenir store (5 Boulevard du Palais) across the street from the Sainte-Chapelle entrance.

Notre-Dame Cathedral: Cathedral—free, Mon-Sat 7:45-18:45, Sun 7:15-19:15; Treasury—€5, not covered by Museum Pass, Mon-Fri 9:30-18:00, Sat 9:30-18:30, Sun 13:30-18:40; audioguide—€5, free English tours—normally Mon, Tue, and Sat at 14:30, Wed and Thu at 14:00.

The cathedral hosts **Mass** several times daily (early morning, noon, and evening), plus Vespers at 17:45. For a schedule of services and summer night spectacles, call or check the website. Tel. 01 42 34 56 10, www.notredamedeparis.fr.

Tower Climb: Entrance for Notre-Dame's tower climb is outside the church, on the left side. It's 400 steps up to a gargoyle's-eye view of the cathedral, Seine, and city (€10, covered by Museum Pass, timed-entry ticket required for everyone—same-day reservations only, available starting 7:30 on JeFile app or at ticket machines on-site; daily April-Sept 10:00-18:30, Fri-Sat until 23:00 in July-Aug, Oct-March 10:00-17:30, last entry 45 minutes before closing; tel. 01 53 10 07 00, www.tours-notre-dame-de-paris.fr).

Deportation Memorial: Free, Tue-Sun 10:00-19:00, Oct-March until 17:00, closed Mon year-round, may randomly close at other times, tel. 01 46 33 87 56.

Sainte-Chapelle: €8.50, €13.50 combo-ticket with Conciergerie, covered by Museum Pass, advance tickets available; daily April-Sept 9:00-19:00, Oct-March until 17:00; audioguide-€4.50 (€6 for two), tel. 01 53 40 60 80, www.sainte-chapelle.fr.

Expect long lines to get in. First comes the security line, which no one can skip (security lines shortest first thing—be in line by 9:15, or arrive at 10:00 after the first rush subsides—and on weekends; longest on Tue and any day around 13:00-14:00). Once past security, you'll encounter the ticket-buying line—those with combo-tickets or Museum Passes can skip this queue.

Conciergerie: €8.50, €13.50 combo-ticket with Sainte-Chapelle, covered by Museum Pass, daily 9:30-18:00, tel. 01 53 40 60 80, www.paris-conciergerie.fr.

Avoiding Crowds: This area is most crowded from midmorning to mid-afternoon, especially on Tue (when the Louvre is closed). On weekends, Notre-Dame and many sights can be packed (but, conversely, the security line for Sainte-Chapelle is often shorter). Generally, come early in the morning or as late in the day as possible. To avoid the Sainte-Chapelle lines, it can be worth rearranging the order in which you take this walk: See Sainte-Chapelle first thing in the morning, then walk over to Notre-Dame (five minutes away) to begin this tour.

Tours: ∩ Download my free Paris Historic Walk audio tour.

THE WALK BEGINS

Start at Notre-Dame Cathedral on the island in the Seine River, the physical and historic bull's-eye of your Paris map. The closest Métro stops are Cité, Hôtel de Ville, and St. Michel.

Notre-Dame and Nearby

On the square in front of the cathedral, stand far enough back to take in the whole facade. Find the circular window in the center.

For centuries, the main figure in the Christian pantheon has been Mary, the mother of Jesus. This church is dedicated to "Our Lady" *(Notre Dame),* and there she is, cradling God, right in the heart of the facade, surrounded by the halo of the rose window.

Notre-Dame—a 200-year construction project

Rose window framing "Our Lady"

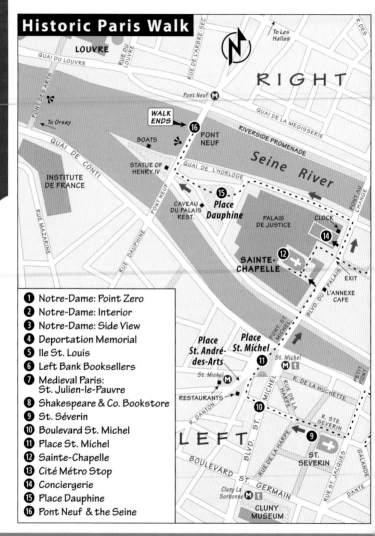

Historic Paris Walk

LOUVRE

QUAI DU LOUVRE

RUE DU LOUVRE

RUE DE L'ARBRE-SEC

To Les Halles

R. DES

RIGHT

PONT DES ARTS

To Orsay

QUAI DE CONTI

Pont Neuf Ⓜ

QUAI DE LA MEGISSERIE

WALK ENDS

🔟16

PONT NEUF

RIVERSIDE PROMENADE

Seine River

BOATS

STATUE OF HENRY IV

QUAI DE L'HORLOGE

PONT NEUF

INSTITUTE DE FRANCE

RUE DAUPHINE

RUE MAZARINE

CAVEAU DU PALAIS REST.

🔟15 Place Dauphine

PALAIS DE JUSTICE

PONT AU CHANGE

CLOCK

🔟14

🔟12

SAINTE-CHAPELLE

EXIT

L'ANNEXE CAFE

BLVD. DU PALAIS

Place St. André-des-Arts

Place St. Michel

PONT ST. MICHEL

🔟11 St. Michel Ⓜ 🚋

St. Michel Ⓜ

RESTAURANTS

R. DANTON

BLVD. ST. MICHEL

🔟10

R. DE LA HUCHETTE

RUE DE LA HARPE

PETIT PONT

RUE STE. SEVERIN

🔟9 ST. SEVERIN

RUE ST. JACQUES

GALANDE

DANTE

LEFT

BOULEVARD ST. GERMAIN

Cluny La Sorbonne Ⓜ 🚋

CLUNY MUSEUM

① Notre-Dame: Point Zero
② Notre-Dame: Interior
③ Notre-Dame: Side View
④ Deportation Memorial
⑤ Ile St. Louis
⑥ Left Bank Booksellers
⑦ Medieval Paris: St. Julien-le-Pauvre
⑧ Shakespeare & Co. Bookstore
⑨ St. Séverin
⑩ Boulevard St. Michel
⑪ Place St. Michel
⑫ Sainte-Chapelle
⑬ Cité Métro Stop
⑭ Conciergerie
⑮ Place Dauphine
⑯ Pont Neuf & the Seine

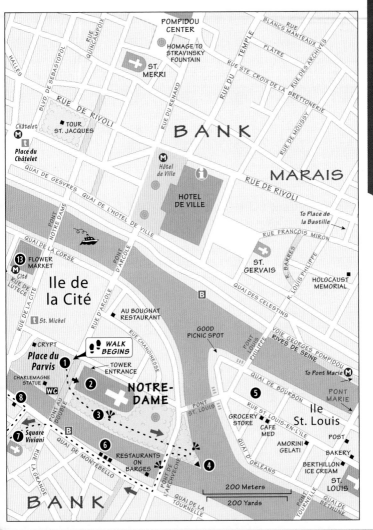

Imagine the faith of the people who built this cathedral. They broke ground in 1163 with the hope that someday their great-great-great-great-great-great grandchildren might attend the dedication Mass, which finally took place two centuries later, in 1345. Look up the 200-foot-tall bell towers and imagine a tiny medieval community mustering the money and energy for construction. Master masons supervised, but the people did much of the grunt work themselves for free—hauling the huge stones from distant quarries, digging a 30-foot-deep trench to lay the foundation, and treading like rats on a wheel designed to lift the stones up, one by one. This kind of backbreaking, arduous manual labor created the real hunchbacks of Notre-Dame.

▶ *"Walk this way" toward the cathedral, and view it from the bronze plaque on the ground (30 yards from the central doorway).*

❶ Point Zero and Notre-Dame

You're standing at the center of France, the point from which all distances are measured. It was also the center of Paris 2,300 years ago, when the Parisii tribe fished where the east-west river crossed a north-south road. The Romans conquered the Parisii and built their Temple of Jupiter where Notre-Dame stands today (52 B.C.). When Rome fell, the Germanic Franks sealed their victory by replacing the temple with the Christian church of St. Etienne in the sixth century.

The grand equestrian statue (to your right, as you face the church) is of Charlemagne ("Charles the Great," 742-814), King of the Franks, whose reign marked the birth of France as a nation.

Before its renovation 150 years ago, this square was much smaller.

Point Zero: Step on the center of France.

Charlemagne, whose "Franks" became "France"

Paris Through History

250 B.C.	Small fishing village of the Parisii, a Celtic tribe.
52 B.C.	Julius Caesar conquers the Parisii capital of Lutetia (near Paris), and the Romans replace it with a new capital on the Left Bank.
A.D. 497	Roman Paris falls to the Germanic Franks. King Clovis (482-511) converts to Christianity and makes Paris his capital.
885-886	Paris gets wasted in a siege by Viking Norsemen = Normans.
1163	Notre-Dame cornerstone laid.
c. 1250	Paris is a bustling commercial city with a university and new construction, such as Sainte-Chapelle and Notre-Dame.
c. 1600	King Henry IV beautifies Paris with buildings, roads, bridges, and squares.
c. 1700	Louis XIV makes Versailles his capital. Parisians grumble.
1789	Paris is the heart of France's Revolution, which condemns thousands to the guillotine.
1804	Napoleon Bonaparte crowns himself emperor in a ceremony at Notre-Dame.
c. 1860	Napoleon's nephew, Napoleon III, builds Paris' wide boulevards.
1889	The centennial of the Revolution is celebrated with the Eiffel Tower. Paris enjoys the prosperity of the belle époque (beautiful age).
1920s	After the draining Great War, Paris is a cheap place to live, attracting expatriates such as Ernest Hemingway.
1940-1944	Occupied Paris spends the war years under gray skies and gray Nazi uniforms.
1981-1995	Paris modernizes: the TGV, the new Louvre Pyramid, Musée d'Orsay, La Grande Arche de la Défense, and Opéra Bastille.
1998	Playing at its home stadium, France wins the World Cup.
2015	A series of terrorist attacks throughout the city tests Parisian resolve.
2016	Great Britain's vote to leave the European Union sends relations between Paris and London into a state of uncertainty.

The church's huge bell towers rose above a tangle of small, ramshackle medieval buildings, inspiring Victor Hugo's story of a deformed bell-ringer who could look down on all of Paris.

Looking two-thirds of the way up Notre-Dame's left tower, those with binoculars or good eyes can find Paris' most photographed gargoyle (see drawing at right). Propped on his elbows on the balcony rail, he watches all the tourists in line.

▸ *Much of Paris' history is right under your feet. Some may consider visiting it in the Archaeological Crypt, a small museum located 100 yards in front of Notre-Dame (✪ for details, see page 148). Otherwise, turn your attention to the rest of the...*

Notre-Dame Facade

▸ *Look at the left doorway, and to the left of the door, find the statue with his head in his hands.*

St. Denis: When Christianity began making converts in Roman Paris, the bishop of Paris, Denis, was beheaded by the Romans. But those early Christians were hard to keep down. Denis simply got up, tucked his head under his arm, headed north, paused at a fountain to wash it off, and continued until he found just the right place to meet his maker. Christianity gained ground, and a church soon replaced the pagan temple.

Last Judgment Relief: Above the central doorway (just under the arches), witness the end of the world. Christ sits on the throne of judgment holding both hands up. Beneath him an angel and a demon weigh souls in the balance; the demon cheats by pressing down. The good souls stand to the left, gazing up to heaven. The bad souls to the right are chained up and led off to a six-hour tour of the Louvre on a hot summer day.

St. Denis with head in hands

Last Judgment (over the central door)

Notre-Dame Facade

- ENTHRALLED TOURISTS
- WOW-WHAT A GREAT VIEW!
- BORED GARGOYLE
- GARGOYLES
- MARY IN ROSE WINDOW
- 28 KINGS OF JUDAH
- ST. DENIS (HOLDING HIS HEAD)
- PORTAL OF MARY
- LAST JUDGMENT
- PORTAL OF ST. ANNE
- Seine River
- To Left Bank & Latin Quarter
- To View Of Flying Buttresses & Deportation Memorial
- PONT AU DOUBLE
- To Right Bank
- TOWER ENTRANCE
- EXIT
- ENTER
- DRINKING FOUNTAIN
- HOTEL DIEU
- POINT ZERO
- WC
- CHARLEMAGNE STATUE
- Place du Parvis
- To Sainte-Chapelle
- To Archaeological Crypt & Place St. Michel

The Kings of Judah: Above the arches is this row of 28 statues. In the days of the French Revolution (1789-1799), these biblical kings were mistaken for the hated French kings, and Notre-Dame represented the oppressive Catholic hierarchy. The citizens stormed the church, crying, "Off with their heads!" Plop—they lopped off the crowned heads of these kings with glee, creating a row of St. Denises that weren't repaired for decades. But the story doesn't end there. A schoolteacher collected the heads and buried them in his backyard for safekeeping. There they slept until 1977, when they were accidentally unearthed. Today, you can stare into the eyes

Notre-Dame's soaring Gothic arches

Joan of Arc—former heretic, now saint

of the original kings in the Cluny Museum, a few blocks away (✪ see page 156).

❷ Notre-Dame Interior

▶ *Enter the church at the right doorway and find a spot where you can view the long, high central aisle. (Be careful: Pickpockets attend church here religiously.)*

Nave

Remove your metaphorical hat and become a simple bareheaded peasant, entering the dim medieval light of the church. Take a minute to let your pupils dilate, then take in the subtle, mysterious light show that God beams through the stained-glass windows. Follow the slender columns up 10 stories to the praying-hands arches of the ceiling, and contemplate the heavens.

This is Gothic. Taller and filled with light, Notre-Dame was a major improvement over the earlier Romanesque style. Gothic architects needed only a few structural columns, topped by crisscrossing pointed arches, to support the weight of the roof. This let them build higher than ever, freeing up the walls for windows.

Notre-Dame has the typical basilica floor plan: a long central nave lined with columns and flanked by side aisles. It's designed in the shape of a cross, with the altar placed where the crossbeam intersects. The church can hold up to 10,000 faithful, and it's probably buzzing with visitors now, just as it was 600 years ago.

Altar

This marks the place where Mass is said and the bread and wine of

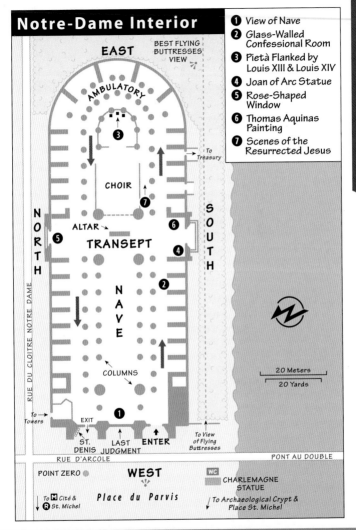

Notre-Dame Interior

EAST

BEST FLYING BUTTRESSES VIEW

AMBULATORY

3

To Treasury

CHOIR

7

N O R T H

5

ALTAR

TRANSEPT

6

4

S O U T H

2

N A V E

COLUMNS

RUE DU CLOITRE NOTRE DAME

20 Meters
20 Yards

1

To Towers

EXIT

ST. DENIS   LAST JUDGMENT   **ENTER**

To View of Flying Buttresses

RUE D'ARCOLE

PONT AU DOUBLE

POINT ZERO

WEST

WC   CHARLEMAGNE STATUE

To **M** Cité & **R** St. Michel

Place du Parvis

To Archaeological Crypt & Place St. Michel

Legend:
1. View of Nave
2. Glass-Walled Confessional Room
3. Pietà Flanked by Louis XIII & Louis XIV
4. Joan of Arc Statue
5. Rose-Shaped Window
6. Thomas Aquinas Painting
7. Scenes of the Resurrected Jesus

Original rose window in north transept

A scene depicting the resurrection of Jesus

Communion are blessed and distributed. In olden days, there were no chairs. This was the holy spot for Romans, Christians...and even atheists during the Revolution. France today, though nominally Catholic, remains aloof from Vatican dogmatism. Instead of traditional wooden confessional booths, there's an inviting **glass-walled room** (right aisle), where modern sinners seek counseling as much as forgiveness.

Just past the altar is the so-called choir, the area enclosed with carved-wood walls, where more intimate services can be held in this spacious building.

Right Transept (and Beyond)

A statue of **Joan of Arc** (Jeanne d'Arc, 1412-1431), dressed in armor and praying, honors the French teenager who rallied her country's soldiers to try to drive English invaders from Paris. The English and their allies burned her at the stake for claiming to hear heavenly voices. Almost immediately, Parisians rallied to condemn Joan's execution, and finally, in 1909, here in Notre-Dame, the former "witch" was beatified.

Join the statue in gazing up to the blue-and-purple, **rose-shaped window** in the opposite transept—with teeny green Mary and baby Jesus in the center—the only one of the three rose windows still with its original medieval glass.

A large painting back down to your right shows portly **Thomas Aquinas** (1225-1274) teaching, while his students drink from the fountain of knowledge. This Italian monk did undergrad and master's work at the multicultural University of Paris, then taught there for several years while writing his theological works. His "scholasticism" used Aristotle's logic to examine the Christian universe, aiming to fuse faith and reason.

> *Continue toward the far end of the church, pausing at the top of the three stairs.*

Circling the Choir

The back side of the choir walls feature **scenes of the resurrected Jesus** (c. 1350) appearing to his followers, starting with Mary Magdalene. The nearby **Treasury** contains lavish robes, golden reliquaries, and the humble tunic of King (and St.) Louis IX, but it probably isn't worth the entry fee.

Surrounding the choir are chapels, each dedicated to a particular saint and funded by a certain guild. One chapel displays models of the church and an exhibit on medieval construction techniques—pulleys, wagons, hamster-wheel cranes, and lots of elbow grease. Throughout the church, the faithful can pause at any of the chapels to light a candle as an offering and meditate in the cool light of the stained glass.

> *Amble around the ambulatory, spill back outside, and make a slow U-turn left. Enter the park (named "Square Jean XXIII") through the iron gates along the riverside and walk about 50 yards until you come to a statue of Saint John Paul II.*

❸ Notre-Dame Side View

Alongside the church you'll notice the flying buttresses. These 50-foot stone "beams" that stick out of the church were the key to the complex Gothic architecture. The pointed arches we saw inside cause the weight of the roof to push outward rather than downward. The "flying" buttresses support the roof by pushing back inward, opening the walls for stained-glass windows.

The gargoyles at the base of the roof stick out from pillars and

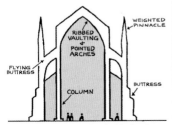

It takes 13 tourists to build a Gothic church: one steeple, six columns, and six buttresses.

buttresses, representing souls caught between heaven and earth. They also function as rainspouts (from the same French root word as "gargle").

The Neo-Gothic 300-foot spire is a product of the 1860 reconstruction of the dilapidated old church. Find the restoration's chief architect, Eugène-Emmanuel Viollet-le-Duc, at the base of the spire among the green apostles and evangelists (visible as you approach the back end of the church), looking up, marveling at his fine work.

▸ *Behind Notre-Dame, cross the street and enter the park at the tip of the island. (If this gate is closed, you can still enter the park 30 yards to the left.) Look for the stairs and head down to reach the...*

❹ Deportation Memorial

This memorial to the 200,000 French victims of the Nazi concentration camps (1940-1945) draws you into their experience. France was quickly overrun by Nazi Germany, and Paris spent the war years under Nazi occupation. Jews and dissidents were rounded up and deported—many never returned.

As you descend the steps, the city around you disappears. Surrounded by walls, you have become a prisoner. Inside, the hallway is lined with 200,000 lighted crystals, one for each French citizen who died. Flickering at the far end is the eternal flame of hope. Above the exit as you leave is the message you'll find at other Holocaust sites: "Forgive, but never forget."

▸ *Back on street level, but before leaving the memorial park, look across the river (north) to the island called...*

❺ Ile St. Louis

If the Ile de la Cité is a tugboat laden with the history of Paris, it's towing this classy little residential dinghy, laden only with high-rent apartments, boutiques, characteristic restaurants, and famous ice cream shops. Consider taking a brief detour across the pedestrian bridge, Pont St. Louis, to explore this little island (or come back in the evening).

▸ *From the Deportation Memorial, cross the bridge to the Left Bank. Turn right and walk along the river, toward the front end of Notre-Dame and to the next bridge. This side view of the church from across the river is one of Europe's great sights and is best from river level.*

Deportation Memorial's 200,000 points of light

Booksellers line the Seine River.

LEFT BANK

❻ Left Bank Booksellers

The Rive Gauche, or the Left Bank of the Seine—"left" if you were float-ing downstream—still has many of the twisting lanes and narrow build-ings of medieval times. The Right Bank is more modern and business-oriented, with wide boulevards and stressed Parisians in suits. Here along the riverbank, the "big business" is secondhand books, displayed in the green metal stalls on the parapet (called *bouquinistes*). With flexible hours and virtually no overhead, they run their businesses as they have since the mid-1500s. Today, the waiting list to become one of Paris' 250 *bouquinistes* is eight years. Each *bouquiniste* (boo-keen-eest) is allowed four boxes, with rent around €100 per year.

▶ *When you reach the bridge (Pont au Double) that crosses to the front of Notre-Dame, veer left across the street and find a small park called Square Viviani. Angle across the square and pass by Paris' oldest inhab-itant—an acacia tree nicknamed Robinier, after the guy who planted it in 1602. Imagine that this same tree might once have shaded the Sun King, Louis XIV. Leave the park, walking past the small rough-stone church of St. Julien-le-Pauvre, to tiny Rue Galande.*

❼ Medieval Paris

Picture Paris in 1250, when the church of St. Julien-le-Pauvre was still new. Notre-Dame was nearly done (so they thought), Sainte-Chapelle had just opened, the university was expanding human knowledge, and Paris was fast becoming a prosperous industrial and commercial center. The area around the church and along Rue Galande gives you some of the medieval feel of ramshackle architecture and old houses leaning every which way. In medieval days, people were piled on top of each other, building at all angles, as they scrambled for this prime real estate near the main commercial artery of the day—the Seine. The smell of fish competed with the smell of neighbors in this knot of humanity.

▶ *Return toward the river and turn left on Rue de la Bûcherie to find…*

❽ Shakespeare and Company Bookstore

In addition to hosting butchers and fishmongers, the Left Bank has been home to scholars, philosophers, and poets since medieval times. This funky bookstore—a reincarnation of the original shop from the 1920s on Rue de l'Odéon—has picked up the literary torch. Sylvia Beach, an American with a passion for free thinking, opened Shakespeare and Company for the post-WWI Lost Generation, who came to Paris to find themselves. American writers flocked to the city for the cheap rent, fleeing the uptight, Prohibition-era United States. Beach's bookstore was famous as a meeting place for the likes of Ernest Hemingway, Gertrude Stein, and Ezra Pound. James Joyce struggled to find a publisher for his now-classic novel *Ulysses*—until Sylvia Beach published it.

▶ *Continue to Rue du Petit-Pont and turn left. This bustling north-south boulevard (which becomes Rue St. Jacques) was the Romans' busiest street 2,000 years ago, with chariots racing in and out of the city. A block south of the Seine, turn right at the Gothic church of St. Séverin and walk into the Latin Quarter.*

❾ Latin Quarter

Don't ask me why, but St. Séverin church took a century longer than

St. Julien-le-Pauvre and 400-year-old tree

This bookstore carries on expatriate bohemian life.

St. Séverin flickers with flamboyant flames.   The Latin Quarter looks "Greek" today.

building Notre-Dame. This is Flamboyant, or "flame-like," Gothic, and you can see how the short, prickly spires are meant to make this building flicker in the eyes of the faithful. The church gives us a close-up look at gargoyles, the decorative drain spouts that also functioned to keep evil spirits away. At #22 Rue St. Séverin, you'll find the skinniest house in Paris, two windows wide.

Although it may look more like the Greek Quarter today (cheap gyros abound), this area is the Latin Quarter, named for the language you'd have heard on these streets if you walked them in the Middle Ages. The University of Paris (founded 1215), one of the leading educational institutions of medieval Europe, was (and still is) nearby.

Walking along Rue St. Séverin, note how the street slopes into a central channel of bricks. In the days before plumbing and toilets, when people still went to the river or neighborhood wells for their water, flushing meant throwing it out the window. At certain times of day, maids on the fourth floor would holler, "Garde de l'eau!" ("Watch out for the water!") and heave it into the streets, where it would eventually wash down into the Seine.

Until the 19th century, all of Paris was like this—a medieval tangle of small streets. The ethnic feel of this area is nothing new—it's been a melting pot and university district for almost 800 years.

▶ Keep wandering straight, and you'll come to...

⑩ Boulevard St. Michel

Busy Boulevard St. Michel (or "boul' Miche") is famous as the main artery for Paris' café and arts scene, culminating a block away (to the left) at the intersection with Boulevard St. Germain. Although nowadays you're more

Eateries Along This Walk

The following spots make for a nice lunch or snack break (✪ see the map on page 18).

Au Bougnat: Local hangout a block north of Notre-Dame, where cops and workers get sandwiches, coffee, and €15 *formules* (a.k.a., two-course *menus*; 26 Rue Chanoinesse).

Ile St. Louis: Stop for gelato at Berthillon or Amorino Gelati, or for crêpes and a view at the recommended Café Med.

Barges in the Seine: Docked near Notre-Dame are barges, some housing cafés with stunning views.

Place St. André-des-Arts: Two nice outdoor restaurants sit amid the bustle on this tree-filled square near Place St. Michel.

L'Annexe Café: Coffee shop across from Sainte-Chapelle's entrance.

Place Dauphine: A few peaceful food refuges can be found on this dreamy square.

likely to find pantyhose at 30 percent off, there are still many cafés, boutiques, and bohemian haunts nearby.

The Sorbonne—the University of Paris' humanities department—is also nearby, if you want to make a detour, though visitors are not allowed to enter. (Turn left on Boulevard St. Michel and walk two blocks south. Gaze at the dome from the Place de la Sorbonne courtyard.) Originally founded as a theological school, the Sorbonne expanded to include other subjects. Nonconformity is a tradition here, and Paris remains a world center for new intellectual trends.

▶ *Cross Boulevard St. Michel. Just ahead is a tiny tree-lined square called Place St. André-des-Arts. Adjoining this square toward the river is the triangular Place St. Michel, with a Métro stop and a statue of St. Michael killing a devil.*

⓫ Place St. Michel

You're standing at the traditional core of the Left Bank's artsy, liberal, hippie, bohemian district of poets, philosophers, winos, and *baba cools* (neo-hippies). Nearby, you'll find international eateries, far-out bookshops, street singers, pale girls in black berets, jazz clubs, and—these days—tourists.

The neighborhood abounds with cafés. For centuries these have been social watering holes, where you can get a warm place to sit and stimulating conversation for the price of a cup of coffee. Every great French writer—from Voltaire and Jean-Jacques Rousseau to Jean-Paul Sartre and Jacques Derrida—had a favorite haunt.

In less commercial times, Place St. Michel was a gathering point for the city's malcontents and misfits. In 1830, 1848, and again in 1871, the citizens took the streets from the government troops, set up barricades *Les Miz*-style, and fought against royalist oppression. During World War II, the locals rose up against their Nazi oppressors (read the plaques under the dragons at the foot of the St. Michel fountain). In the spring of 1968, a time of social upheaval all over the world, young students battled riot batons and tear gas by digging up the cobblestones on the street and hurling them at police. They took over the square and declared it an independent state, forcing change. Demonstrations still take place here, but the cobblestones have been replaced with pavement, so scholars can never again use the streets as weapons.

▶ *From Place St. Michel, head for the prickly steeple of Sainte-Chapelle. Cross the river on Pont St. Michel and continue north along the Boulevard du Palais until you reach the doorway (on your left).*

⑫ Sainte-Chapelle

Security is strict at the Sainte-Chapelle complex because this is more than a tourist attraction: France's Supreme Court meets to the right of Sainte-Chapelle in the Palais de Justice. Once past security, you'll enter the

Place St. Michel, where revolutionaries gather

Sainte-Chapelle—built for the Crown of Thorns

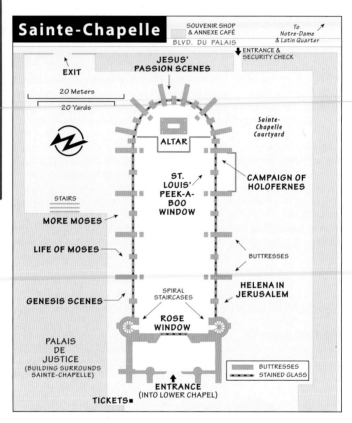

Sainte-Chapelle

SOUVENIR SHOP
& ANNEXE CAFÉ

To
Notre-Dame
& Latin Quarter

BLVD. DU PALAIS

ENTRANCE &
SECURITY CHECK

EXIT

JESUS'
PASSION SCENES

20 Meters

20 Yards

Sainte-
Chapelle
Courtyard

ALTAR

ST.
LOUIS'
PEEK-A-
BOO
WINDOW

CAMPAIGN OF
HOLOFERNES

STAIRS

MORE MOSES

LIFE OF MOSES

BUTTRESSES

GENESIS SCENES

SPIRAL
STAIRCASES

HELENA IN
JERUSALEM

ROSE
WINDOW

PALAIS
DE
JUSTICE
(BUILDING SURROUNDS
SAINTE-CHAPELLE)

BUTTRESSES
STAINED GLASS

ENTRANCE
(INTO LOWER CHAPEL)

TICKETS ▪

courtyard outside Sainte-Chapelle, where you'll find information about up-coming church concerts. The ticket office is near the church entry, which is often hidden behind a long line of ticket buyers (those with a Museum Pass or Conciergerie combo-ticket can march to the front and be allowed right in).

This triumph of Gothic church architecture is a cathedral of glass like no other. It was speedily built between 1242 and 1248 for King Louis IX—the only French king who is now a saint—to house the supposed

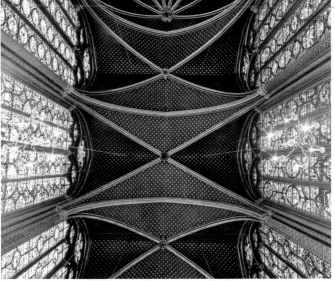

Ste.-Chapelle's crisscross arches and slim columns make the walls of stained glass possible.

Crown of Thorns. Its architectural harmony is due to the fact that it was completed under the direction of one architect and in only six years—unheard of in Gothic times. Recall that Notre-Dame took more than 200 years.

Though the inside is beautiful, the exterior is basically functional. The muscular buttresses hold up the stone roof, so the walls are essentially there to display stained glass. The lacy spire is Neo-Gothic—added in the 19th century.

▶ *Climb the spiral staircase to the Chapelle Haute. Leave the rough stone of the earth and step into the light.*

The Stained Glass

Fiat lux. "Let there be light." From the first page of the Bible, it's clear: Light is divine. Light shines through stained glass like God's grace shining down to earth. Gothic architects used their new technology to turn dark stone

Stained Glass Supreme

Craftsmen made glass—which is, essentially, melted sand—using this recipe:

- Melt one part sand with two parts wood ash.
- Mix in rusty metals to get different colors—iron makes red; cobalt makes blue; copper, green; manganese, purple; cadmium, yellow.
- Blow glass into a cylinder shape, cut lengthwise, and lay flat to cool.
- Cut into pieces with an iron tool, or by heating and cooling a select spot to make it crack.
- Fit pieces together to form a figure, using strips of lead to hold them in place.
- Place masterpiece so high on a wall that no one can read it.

buildings into lanterns of light. The glory of Gothic shines brighter here than in any other church.

There are 15 separate panels of stained glass (6,500 square feet—two thirds of it 13th-century original), with more than 1,100 different scenes, mostly from the Bible. These cover the entire Christian history of the world, from the Creation in Genesis (first window on the left, as you face the altar), to the coming of Christ (over the altar), to the end of the world (the round "rose"-shaped window at the rear of the church). Each individual scene is interesting, and the whole effect is overwhelming. Allow yourself a few minutes to bask in the glow of the colored light before tackling the window descriptions below.

▶ *Working clockwise from the entrance, look for these notable scenes. (The sun lights up different windows at various times of day. Overcast days give the most even light. On bright, sunny days, some sections are glorious, while others look like sheets of lead.)*

Genesis—Cain Clubbing Abel (first window on the left, always dark because of a building butted up against it): On the bottom level in the third circle from the left, we see God create the round earth and hold it up. On the next level up, we catch glimpses of naked Adam and Eve. On the third level (far right circle), Cain, in red, clubs his brother Abel, committing the first murder.

Life of Moses (second window, the dark bottom row of diamond panels): The first panel shows baby Moses in a basket, placed by his sister in the squiggly brown river. Next he's found by the pharaoh's daughter. Then he grows up. And finally, he's a man, a prince of Egypt on his royal throne.

Jesus' Passion Scenes (directly over the altar and behind the canopy): These scenes from Jesus' arrest and Crucifixion were the backdrop for the Crown of Thorns (originally displayed on the altar), which was placed on Jesus' head when the Romans were torturing and humiliating him before his execution. Stand close to the steps of the altar and look through the canopy to see Jesus, tied to a green column, being whipped. Alongside is the key scene in this relic chapel—Jesus (in purple robe) being fitted with the painful Crown of Thorns. Just below the top of the canopy, find Jesus in yellow shorts, carrying his cross (fifth frame up from right bottom).

Campaign of Holofernes (window to the right of the altar wall): On the bottom row are four scenes of colorful knights. The second circle from the left is a battle scene (the campaign of Holofernes), showing three soldiers with swords slaughtering three men.

Notice the intricate details the glass-makers have created in this difficult medium. The background is blue. The men have different-colored clothes—red, blue, green, mauve, and white. You can see the folds in the robes, the hair, and facial features. The victim in the center has his head splotched with blood. Such details were created by scratching on the glass or baking on paint. It was a painstaking process of finding just the right colors, fitting them together to make a scene...and then multiplying by 1,100.

Rose Window (above entrance): It's Judgment Day, with a tiny Christ in the center of the chaos and miracles.

Campaign of Holofernes, one detail of many

Altar for the Crown of Thorns

Altar

The altar was raised up high to better display the Crown of Thorns, the relic around which this chapel was built. Notice the staircase: Access was limited to the priest and the king, who wore the keys to the shrine around his neck.

King Louis IX, convinced he'd found the real McCoy, spent roughly the equivalent of €500 million for the Crown, €370 million for the gem-studded shrine to display it in (later destroyed in the French Revolution), and a mere €150 million to build Sainte-Chapelle to house it. Today, the supposed Crown of Thorns is kept by the Notre-Dame Treasury (though it's occasionally brought out for display).

Lay your camera on the ground and shoot the ceiling. Those pure and simple ribs growing out of the slender columns are the essence of Gothic structure.

▶ *Exit Sainte-Chapelle. Back outside, walk counterclockwise around the church to reach the street. You'll pass the giant* **Palais de Justice,** *now the home of the French Supreme Court. The motto "Liberté, Egalité, Fraternité" over the doors is a reminder that this was also the head-quarters of the Revolutionary government. Here they doled out justice, condemning many to imprisonment in the Conciergerie downstairs—or to the guillotine.*

Pass through the big iron gate to the noisy Boulevard du Palais. Cross the street to the wide, pedestrian-only Rue de Lutèce and walk about halfway down to see the ⓭ **Cité "Metropolitain"** *Métro stop, with one of the few original subway entrances that survives (early-20th-century; preserved as a national art treasure for its curvy, plantlike Art Nouveau ironwork).*

From the Palais de Justice, head north a few steps on Boulevard du Palais, and enter the Conciergerie (passholders can sidestep the bottle-neck created by the ticket-buying line).

⓮ Conciergerie

Positioned next to the courthouse, the Conciergerie was the gloomy pris-on famous as the last stop for 2,780 victims of the guillotine, including France's last *ancien régime* queen, Marie-Antoinette.

Inside, pick up a free map and breeze through. See the spacious, low-ceilinged Hall of Men-at-Arms (Room 1), originally a guards' din-ing room. Pass through the bookstore to find the Office of the Keeper,

The Conciergerie—a photogenic torture chamber—held prisoners awaiting the guillotine.

Original Art Nouveau Métro entrance

Marie-Antoinette's cell in the Conciergerie

or "Concierge" of the place (who admitted shackled prisoners, monitored torture...and recommended nearby restaurants). Next door is the *Toilette,* where condemned prisoners combed their hair or touched up their lipstick before their final public appearance—waiting for the open-air cart (tumbrel) to pull up outside and carry them to the guillotine (on Place de la Concorde).

Upstairs is a memorial room with the names of the 2,780 citizens condemned to death by the guillotine. Here are some of the people you'll find. Charlotte Corday *("dite d'Armais"),* a noblewoman, snuck into the bathroom of the revolutionary writer Jean-Paul Marat and stabbed him while he bathed. Georges Danton was a prominent revolutionary who was later condemned for being insufficiently liberal—a nasty crime. Louis XVI (called "Capet: Last King of France") deserves only a modest mention, as does his wife, Marie-Antoinette. And finally—oh, the irony—there's Maximilien de Robespierre, the head of the Revolution, the man who sent so many to the guillotine. He was eventually toppled, humiliated, imprisoned here, and beheaded.

Back downstairs, you eventually arrive at a re-creation of Marie-Antoinette's cell. Imagine the queen spending her last days—separated from her 10-year-old son, and now widowed because the king had already been executed. Mannequins, period furniture, and the real cell wallpaper set the scene. The guard stands modestly behind a screen, while the queen psyches herself up with a crucifix. On October 16, 1793, the queen stepped onto the cart and was slowly carried to Place de la Concorde, where she had a date with "Monsieur de Paris."

▶ *Back outside, turn left on Boulevard du Palais. On the corner is the city's oldest public clock, from 1334. Turn left onto Quai de l'Horloge*

*and walk along the river. The bridge up ahead is the Pont Neuf, where
we'll end this walk. At the first corner, veer left into a sleepy triangular
square called...*

⓯ Place Dauphine

It's amazing to find such coziness in the heart of Paris. This city of more
than two million is still a city of neighborhoods, a collection of villages. The
French Supreme Court building looms behind like a giant marble gavel.
Enjoy the village-Paris feeling in the park and consider a break at the refined
$$$ Caveau du Palais restaurant or the funky $$ Ma Salle à Manger.

▶ *Continue through Place Dauphine. As you pop out the other end, you're
face-to-face with a statue of Henry IV (1553-1610). Though not as famous
as his grandson, Louis XIV, Henry helped make Paris what it is today—a
European capital of elegant buildings (the Louvre's Grand Gallery), quiet
squares (Place Dauphine), and majestic bridges (Pont Neuf, to your right).
Walk onto the bridge and pause at the little nook halfway across.*

Pont Neuf—400-year old "new bridge"

⑯ Pont Neuf and the Seine

This "new bridge" is now Paris' oldest. Built during Henry IV's reign (about 1600), its arches span the widest part of the river. Unlike other bridges, this one never had houses or buildings growing on it. The turrets were originally for vendors and street entertainers. From the bridge, look downstream (west) to see the next bridge, the pedestrian-only Pont des Arts. Ahead on the Right Bank is the long Louvre museum. Beyond that, on the Left Bank, is the Orsay. And what's that tall black tower in the distance?

Our walk ends where Paris began—on the Seine River. From Dijon to the English Channel, the Seine meanders 500 miles, cutting through the center of Paris. The river is shallow and slow within the city, but still dangerous enough to require steep stone embankments (built 1910) to prevent occasional floods.

In summer, the roads that run along the river are decked out with potted palm trees, hammocks, beach chairs, and tanned locals, creating the *Paris Plages* (Paris Beaches). Any time of year, you'll see tourist boats and the commercial barges that carry 20 percent of Paris' transported goods. And on the banks, sportsmen today cast into the waters once fished by Paris' original Celtic inhabitants.

▶ *We're done. You can take a boat tour that leaves from near the base of Pont Neuf on the island side (Vedettes du Pont Neuf). The nearest Métro stop is Pont Neuf, across the bridge on the Right Bank. Bus #69 heads east along Quai du Louvre (at the north end of the bridge) and west along Rue de Rivoli (a block farther north). In fact, you can go anywhere—you're standing in the heart of Paris.*

Louvre Tour

Musée du Louvre

Paris' world-class museums walk you through world history, and the best place to start your "art-yssey" is at the Louvre. With more than 30,000 works of art, the Louvre is a full inventory of Western civilization. To cover it all in one visit is impossible. Let's focus on the Louvre's specialties—Greek sculpture, Italian painting, and French painting.

We'll see "Venuses" through history, from prehistoric stick figures to the curvy *Venus de Milo* to the wind-blown *Winged Victory of Samothrace,* and from placid medieval Madonnas to the *Mona Lisa* to the symbol of modern democracy. Each generation defined beauty differently, and we'll gain insight into long-ago civilizations by admiring what they found beautiful.

ORIENTATION

Cost: €15, free on first Sun of month Oct-March, covered by Museum Pass. Tickets good all day; reentry allowed.

Hours: Wed-Mon 9:00-18:00, Wed and Fri until 21:45, closed Tue, last entry 45 minutes before closing.

When to Go: Crowds can be miserably bad on Sun, Mon (the worst day), Wed, and in the morning (arrive 30 minutes before opening to secure a good place in line). Evening visits are quieter.

Buying Tickets at the Louvre: Self-serve ticket machines located under the pyramid may be faster to use than the ticket windows (machines accept euro bills, coins, and chip-and-PIN Visa cards). A shop in the underground mall sells tickets and Museum Passes, for no extra charge (cash only).

Getting There: Métro stop Palais Royal-Musée du Louvre is the closest. The eastbound bus #69 stops along the Seine River; the best stop is labeled Quai François Mitterrand. The westbound #69 stops in front of the pyramid. You'll find a taxi stand on Rue de Rivoli, next to the Palais Royal-Musée du Louvre Métro station.

Getting In: There is no grander entry than through the **main entrance** at the pyramid in the central courtyard, but lines (for security reasons) can be long. Passholders have a queue that puts them near the head of the security line.

Anyone can enter the Louvre from its less crowded **underground entrance,** accessed through the Carrousel du Louvre shopping mall. Enter the mall at 99 Rue de Rivoli (the door with the red awning) or directly from the Métro stop Palais Royal-Musée du Louvre

Main pyramid entrance

The underground mall entrance is less crowded.

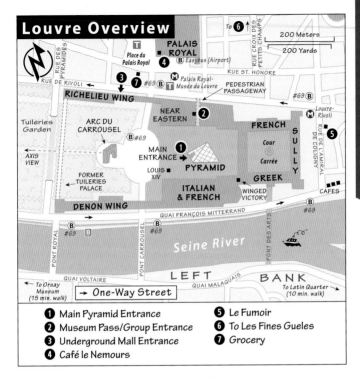

Louvre Overview

To **6** ↑

200 Meters
200 Yards

PALAIS ROYAL

Place du Palais Royal **4**

Ⓑ *Easybus (Airport)*

RUE ST. HONORE

Ⓣ
Ⓣ

3 **7** #69 Ⓑ Ⓣ

Ⓜ Palais Royal-
Musée du Louvre

RUE DE RIVOLI ←

RICHELIEU WING

PEDESTRIAN PASSAGEWAY

#69 Ⓑ →

NEAR EASTERN ■ **2**

Louvre-Rivoli Ⓜ

Tuileries Garden

ARC DU CARROUSEL

FRENCH

Ⓑ#69

Cour Carrée

SULLY

5

AXIS VIEW ←

MAIN ENTRANCE →

PYRAMID **1**

GREEK

FORMER TUILERIES PALACE

LOUIS XIV

ITALIAN & FRENCH

WINGED VICTORY →

CAFES

DENON WING

QUAI FRANÇOIS MITTERRAND

Ⓑ #69

Ⓑ #69
Ⓑ

Ⓑ #69

PONT ROYAL

PONT CARROUSEL

Seine River

PONT DES ARTS

QUAI VOLTAIRE

LEFT

QUAI MALAQUAIS

BANK

← To Orsay Museum (15 min. walk)

→ One-Way Street

To Latin Quarter → (10 min. walk)

1 Main Pyramid Entrance
2 Museum Pass/Group Entrance
3 Underground Mall Entrance
4 Café le Nemours
5 Le Fumoir
6 To Les Fines Gueles
7 Grocery

(stepping off the train, take the exit to *Musée du Louvre-Le Carrousel du Louvre*). Museum Pass holders can sometimes skip to the head of the security line, but if that special line is not obvious, don't bother following signs pointing you to the *Pyramid Passholders* entrance (which is a long detour away).

Information: Tel. 01 40 20 53 17, recorded info tel. 01 40 20 51 51, www.louvre.fr.

Tours: Ninety-minute English-language guided tours leave twice daily (except the first Sun of the month Oct-March) from the *Accueil des Groupes* area, under the pyramid (normally at 11:15 and 14:00, possibly more often in summer; €12 plus admission, tour tel. 01 40 20 52 63). Videoguides (€5) provide commentary on about 700 masterpieces.

🎧 Download my free Louvre Museum audio tour.

Length of This Tour: Allow at least two hours.

Baggage Check: You can store bags for free in self-service lockers (look for the *Vestiaires* sign). Bigger bags must be checked.

Services: WCs are located under the pyramid. Once you're in the galleries, WCs are scarce.

Photography: Photography without a flash is allowed.

Cuisine Art: The Louvre has several cafés. The best is $$ Café Mollien, near the end of our tour (on the terrace overlooking the pyramid, closes at 18:00). A self-service $ cafeteria is up the escalator from the pyramid in the Richelieu wing. $$$ Le Grand Louvre Café under the pyramid is a pricier option. For the best selection, walk to the underground shopping mall, the Carrousel du Louvre, which has a food court upstairs with decent-value, multiethnic fast-food eateries. Outside the Louvre, try the venerable $$ Café le Nemours or the classy $$$ Le Fumoir, or picnic in the Palais Royal gardens (✪ see page 186).

Quick Tips: Expect changes to this tour, as the sprawling Louvre is constantly shuffling its deck. Rooms close, and pieces can be on loan or in restoration. Zero in on the biggies, and try to finish the tour with enough energy left to browse.

Starring: *Venus de Milo, Winged Victory, Mona Lisa,* Leonardo da Vinci, Raphael, Michelangelo, the French painters, and many of the most iconic images of Western civilization.

THE TOUR BEGINS

▶ *Start by picking up a free map at the information desk and and orienting yourself while standing underneath the glass pyramid.*

The Louvre, the largest museum in the Western world, fills three wings of this immense, U-shaped palace. The **Richelieu wing** (north side) houses Near Eastern Antiquities, decorative arts, and French, German, and Northern European art. The **Sully wing** (east side) has extensive French painting and collections of ancient Egyptian and Greek art. We'll concentrate on the Louvre's south side: the **Denon** and **Sully** wings, which hold many of the superstars, including ancient Greek sculpture, Italian Renaissance painting, and French Neoclassical and Romantic painting.

▶ *From the pyramid, head for the Denon wing. Ride the escalator up one floor. After showing your ticket, continue ahead 25 paces, take the first left, follow the* Antiquités Grecques *signs, and climb a set of stairs to the brick-ceilinged Salle (Room) 1: Grèce Préclassique. Enter prehistory.*

GREECE (3000 B.C.-A.D. 1)

Pre-Classical Greek Statues
These statues are noble but crude. In the first glass cases, find Greek Barbie dolls (3000 B.C.) that are older than the pyramids. These prerational voodoo dolls whittle women down to their life-giving traits. Halfway down

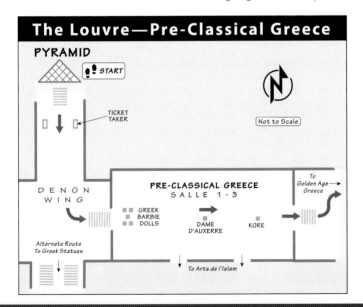

The Louvre—Pre-Classical Greece

the hall, a miniature woman *(Dame d'Auxerre)* pledges allegiance to stability. Nearby, another woman *(Core)* is essentially a column with breasts. These statues stand like they have a gun to their backs—hands at sides, facing front, with sketchy muscles and mask-like faces. "Don't move." The early Greeks, who admired statues like these, found stability more attractive than movement.

But around 450 B.C., Greece entered its Golden Age, a cultural explosion that changed the course of history. Over the next 500 years, Greece produced art that was rational, orderly, and balanced. The balance between timeless stability and fleeting movement made beauty. Most of the art that we'll see in the Louvre either came from or was inspired by Greece.

▶ *Let's head for one of the ancient world's finest statues. Exit at the far end of the pre-Classical Greece galleries, and climb the stairs one flight. At the top, veer left (toward 11 o'clock), and continue into the Sully wing. After about 50 yards, turn right into Salle 16, where you'll find* Venus de Milo *floating above a sea of worshipping tourists. It's been said that among the warlike Greeks, this was the first statue to unilaterally disarm.*

Venus de Milo, a.k.a. *Aphrodite,* late 2nd century B.C.

This goddess of love created a sensation when it was discovered in 1820 on the Greek island of Melos. Europe was already in the grip of a classical fad, and this statue seemed to sum up all that ancient Greece stood for. The optimistic Greeks pictured their gods in human form (meaning humans are godlike), and *Venus'* well-proportioned body captures the balance and orderliness of the Greek universe.

Venus de Milo—balance of opposites

Athena in the Gallery of Statues

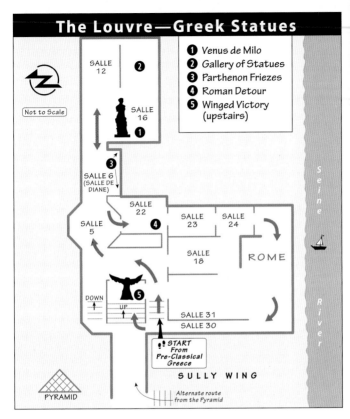

The Louvre—Greek Statues

❶ Venus de Milo
❷ Gallery of Statues
❸ Parthenon Friezes
❹ Roman Detour
❺ Winged Victory (upstairs)

Not to Scale

SALLE 12

SALLE 16

SALLE 6 (SALLE DE DIANE)

SALLE 22

SALLE 5

SALLE 23 SALLE 24

SALLE 18

ROME

DOWN

UP

SALLE 31
SALLE 30

START From Pre-Classical Greece

SULLY WING

PYRAMID

Alternate route from the Pyramid

Seine River

Split *Venus* down the middle from nose to toes and see how the two halves balance each other. *Venus* rests on her right foot (a position called *contrapposto,* or "counterpoise"), then lifts her left leg, setting her whole body in motion. As the left leg rises, her right shoulder droops down. And as her knee points one way, her head turns the other, giving a balanced S-curve to her body (especially noticeable from the back). *Venus* is a harmonious balance of opposites, orbiting slowly around a vertical axis.

Other opposites balance as well, like the smooth skin of her upper half that sets off the rough-cut texture of her dress (size 14). She's actually made from two different pieces of stone plugged together at the hips (the seam is visible). The face is realistic and anatomically accurate, but it's also idealized, a goddess, too generic and too perfect. This isn't any particular woman, but Everywoman—all the idealized features that appealed to the Greeks.

What were her missing arms doing? Some say her right arm held her dress, while her left arm was raised. Others say she was hugging a male statue or leaning on a column. I say she was picking her navel.

▶ *Orbit Venus. This statue is interesting and different from every angle. Remember the view from the back—we'll see it again later. Now make your reentry to earth. Follow* Venus' *gaze and browse around the adjoining rooms (15, 14, and 13) of this long hall.*

Gallery of Statues

Greek statues feature the human body in all its splendor. The anatomy is accurate, and the poses are relaxed and natural. Greek sculptors learned to capture people in motion and to show them from different angles, not just face-forward. The classic *contrapposto* pose—with the weight resting on one leg—captures a balance between timeless stability and fleeting motion.

In this gallery, you'll see statues of gods, satyrs, soldiers, athletes, and everyday people engaged in ordinary activities. For Athenians, the most popular goddess was their patron, Athena. She's usually shown as a warrior, wearing a helmet and carrying a (missing) spear, ready to fight for her city. A monumental version of Athena stands at one end of the hall—the goddess of wisdom facing the goddess of love *(Venus de Milo)*. Whatever the statue, Golden Age artists sought the perfect balance between down-to-earth humans (with human flaws and quirks) and the idealized perfection of Greek gods.

▶ *Head to Salle 6 (also known as Salle de Diane), located behind the* Venus de Milo. *(Facing* Venus, *find Salle 6 to your right, back the way you came.) You'll find two carved panels on opposite walls.*

Parthenon Friezes, mid-5th century B.C.

These stone fragments once decorated the exterior of the greatest Athenian temple, the Parthenon, built at the peak of the Greek Golden Age. A model of the Parthenon shows where the panels might have hung. The centaur panel would have gone above the entrance. The panel of young women was placed under the covered colonnade, but above the doorway (to see it in the model, you'll have to crouch way down and look up).

The panel on the right side of the room shows a centaur sexually harassing a woman, telling the story of how these rude creatures crashed a party of regular people. But the humans fought back and threw the brutes out, just as Athens had defeated its Persian invaders.

The other relief shows the sacred procession of young women who marched up the hill every four years with an embroidered shawl for the 40-foot-high statue of Athena, the goddess of wisdom. Carved in only a couple of inches of stone, they're amazingly realistic. They glide along horizontally (their belts and shoulders all in a line), while the folds of their dresses drape down vertically. The man in the center is relaxed, realistic, and *contrapposto*. Notice the veins in his arm. The maidens' pleated dresses make them look as stable as fluted columns, but their arms and legs step out naturally—their human forms emerging gracefully from the stone.

▶ *Keep backtracking another 20 paces, turning left into Salle 22, the Roman Antiquities room (Antiquités Romaines), for a...*

Roman Detour (Salles 22-30)

Stroll among the Caesars and try to see the person behind the public persona. Besides the many faces of the ubiquitous Emperor *Inconnu* ("unknown"), you might spot Augustus (Auguste), the first emperor, and his wily wife, Livia (Livie). Their son Tiberius (Tibère) was the Caesar that Jesus Christ "rendered unto." Caligula was notoriously depraved, curly-haired Domitia murdered her husband, Hadrian popularized the beard, Trajan ruled the Empire at its peak, and Marcus Aurelius (Marc Aurèle) presided stoically over Rome's slow fall.

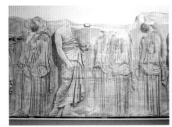
Parthenon frieze—natural movement

Roman busts—warts-and-all realism

The pragmatic Romans (500 B.C.-A.D. 500) were great conquerors but bad artists. One area in which they excelled was realistic portrait busts, especially of their emperors, who were worshipped as gods on earth. The Romans also loved Greek statues and made countless copies, adding a veneer of sophistication to their homes, temples, baths, and government buildings.

▶ *To reach the* Winged Victory *continue clockwise through the Roman collection of sarcophagi and mosaics, which eventually spills out at the base of the stairs leading up to the first floor and the dramatic...*

Winged Victory of Samothrace, c. 190 B.C.

This woman with wings, poised on the prow of a ship, once stood on an island hilltop to commemorate a naval victory. Her clothes are windblown and sea-sprayed, clinging close enough to her body to win a wet T-shirt contest. Originally, her right arm was stretched high, celebrating the victory like a Super Bowl champion, waving a "we're number one" finger.

This is the *Venus de Milo* gone Hellenistic, from the time after the culture of Athens was spread around the Mediterranean by Alexander the Great (c. 325 B.C.). As *Victory* strides forward, the wind blows her and her wings back. Her feet are firmly on the ground, but her wings (and missing arms) stretch upward. She is a pillar of vertical strength, while the clothes curve and whip around her. These opposing forces create a feeling of great energy, making her the lightest two-ton piece of rock in captivity.

In the glass case nearby is *Victory*'s open right hand with an outstretched finger, found in 1950, a century after the statue itself was unearthed. When the French learned the hand was in Turkey, they negotiated with the Turkish government for the rights to it. Considering all the other ancient treasures that France had looted from Turkey in the past, the Turks thought it only appropriate to give the French the finger.

▶ *Enter the octagonal room to the left as you face the* Winged Victory, *with Icarus bungee-jumping from the ceiling. Find a friendly window and look out toward the pyramid.*

The Louvre as a Palace

Formerly a royal palace, the Louvre was built in stages over eight centuries. On your right (the Sully wing) was the original medieval fortress. About 500 yards to the west, in the now-open area past the pyramid and the triumphal arch, is where the Tuileries Palace used to stand. Succeeding kings tried to connect these two palaces, each monarch adding another section onto the long, skinny north and south wings. Finally, in 1852, after three centuries of building, the two palaces were connected, creating a rectangular Louvre. Nineteen years later, the Tuileries Palace burned down during a riot, leaving the U-shaped Louvre we see today.

The glass pyramid was designed by the Chinese-born American architect I. M. Pei (1989). Many Parisians initially hated the pyramid, just as they hated another new and controversial structure 100 years earlier—the Eiffel Tower.

In the octagonal room, find the plaque at the base of the dome. The inscription reads: *"Le Musée du Louvre, fondé le 16 Septembre, 1792."* The museum was founded by France's Revolutionary National Assembly—the same people who brought you the guillotine. What could be more logical? You behead the king, inherit his palace and art collection, open the doors to the masses, and *voilà!* You have Europe's first public museum.

▶ *From the octagonal room, enter the Apollo Gallery (Galerie d'Apollon).*

Apollo Gallery

This gallery gives us a feel for the Louvre as the glorious home of French kings (before Versailles). Imagine a chandelier-lit party in this room, drenched in stucco and gold leaf, with tapestries of leading Frenchmen and paintings featuring mythological and symbolic themes. The crystal vases, the inlaid tables, and many other art objects show the wealth of France, Europe's number-one power for two centuries. Portraits on the walls depict great French kings: Henry IV, who built the Pont Neuf; Louis XIV, the Sun King; and François I, who brought Leonardo da Vinci (and the Italian Renaissance) to France.

Stroll past glass cases of royal dinnerware to the far end of the room. In a glass case are the crown jewels. The display varies, but you

Winged Victory—wind-blown exuberance

Crown jewels in the Apollo Gallery

may see the jewel-studded crown of Louis XV and the less flashy Crown of Charlemagne, along with the 140-carat Regent Diamond, which once graced crowns worn by Louis XV, Louis XVI, and Napoleon.

▶ *A rare WC is a half-dozen rooms away, near Salle 38 in the Sully wing. The Italian collection (Peintures Italiennes) is on the other side of* Winged Victory. *Cross back in front of* Winged Victory *and enter the Denon wing and Salle 1, where you'll find two* **Botticelli frescoes** *that give us a preview of how ancient Greece would be "reborn" in the Renaissance. Now continue into the large Salle 3.*

THE MEDIEVAL WORLD (1200-1500)

Cimabue, *The Madonna and Child in Majesty Surrounded by Angels,* c. 1280

During the Age of Faith (1200s), almost every church in Europe had a painting like this one. Mary was a cult figure—even bigger than the late-20th-century Madonna—adored and prayed to by the faithful for bringing baby Jesus into the world. After the collapse of the Roman Empire (c. A.D. 500), medieval Europe was a poor and violent place, with the Christian Church as the only constant in troubled times.

Altarpieces tended to follow the same formula: somber iconic faces, stiff poses, elegant folds in the robes, and generic angels. Cimabue's holy figures are laid flat on a gold background like cardboard cutouts, existing in a golden never-never land, as though the faithful couldn't imagine them as flesh-and-blood humans inhabiting our dark and sinful earth.

Cimabue—2-D cardboard cutouts

Giotto—hints of 3-D and humanism

Giotto, *St. Francis of Assisi Receiving the Stigmata*, c. 1295-1300

Francis of Assisi (c. 1181-1226), a wandering Italian monk of renowned goodness, kneels on a rocky Italian hillside, pondering the pain of Christ's torture and execution. Suddenly, he looks up, startled, to see Christ himself, with six wings, hovering above. Christ shoots lasers from his wounds to the hands, feet, and side of the empathetic monk, marking him with the stigmata. Francis went on to breathe the spirit of the Renaissance into medieval Europe. His humble love of man and nature inspired artists like Giotto to portray real human beings with real emotions, living in a physical world of beauty.

Like a good filmmaker, Giotto (c. 1266-1337, JOT-toh) doesn't just *tell* us what happened, he *shows* us in the present tense, freezing the scene at its most dramatic moment. Though the perspective is crude—Francis' hut is smaller than he is, and Christ is somehow shooting at Francis while facing us—Giotto creates the illusion of three dimensions, with a foreground (Francis), middle ground (his hut), and background (the hillside). In the predella (the panel of paintings beneath the altarpiece), Francis gives a sermon in the open air, while birds gather at his feet to catch a few words from the beloved hippie of Assisi.

▶ *The long Grand Gallery displays Italian Renaissance painting—some masterpieces, some not.*

ITALIAN RENAISSANCE (1400-1600)

Built in the late 1500s to connect the old palace with the Tuileries Palace, the **Grand Gallery** displays much of the Louvre's Italian Renaissance art. From the doorway, look to the far end and consider this challenge: I hold the world's record for the Grand Gallery Heel-Toe-Fun-Walk-Tourist-Slalom, going end to end in 1 minute, 58 seconds (only two injured). Time yourself. Along the way, notice some of the features of Italian Renaissance painting:

- **Religious:** Lots of Madonnas, children, martyrs, and saints.

- **Symmetrical:** The Madonnas are flanked by saints—two to the left, two to the right, and so on.

- **Realistic:** Real-life human features are especially obvious in the occasional portrait.

The Louvre—Grand Gallery

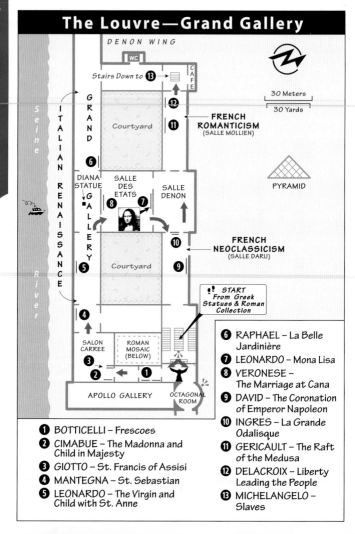

DENON WING

WC

Stairs Down to **13**

CAFE

12

11

FRENCH ROMANTICISM
(SALLE MOLLIEN)

GRAND GALLERY

Courtyard

ITALIAN RENAISSANCE

6

DIANA STATUE

SALLE DES ETATS

SALLE DENON

8   **7**

30 Meters

30 Yards

PYRAMID

5

Courtyard

10

FRENCH NEOCLASSICISM
(SALLE DARU)

9

4

START
From Greek
Statues & Roman
Collection

SALON CARREE

ROMAN MOSAIC
(BELOW)

3

2   **1**

APOLLO GALLERY

OCTAGONAL ROOM

6 RAPHAEL – La Belle Jardinière

7 LEONARDO – Mona Lisa

8 VERONESE – The Marriage at Cana

9 DAVID – The Coronation of Emperor Napoleon

10 INGRES – La Grande Odalisque

11 GERICAULT – The Raft of the Medusa

12 DELACROIX – Liberty Leading the People

13 MICHELANGELO – Slaves

Seine River

1 BOTTICELLI – Frescoes

2 CIMABUE – The Madonna and Child in Majesty

3 GIOTTO – St. Francis of Assisi

4 MANTEGNA – St. Sebastian

5 LEONARDO – The Virgin and Child with St. Anne

A victim of persecution

A victim of the Louvre

• **Three-Dimensional:** Every scene gets a spacious setting with a distant horizon.

• **Classical:** You'll see some Greek gods and classical nudes, but even Christian saints pose like Greek statues, and Mary is a Venus whose face and gestures embody all that was good in the Christian world.

Andrea Mantegna, *St. Sebastian,* c. 1480

Not the patron saint of acupuncture, St. Sebastian was a Christian martyr, although here he looks more like a classical Greek statue. Notice the *contrapposto* stance (all of his weight resting on one leg) and the Greek ruins scattered around him. His executioners look like ignorant medieval brutes bewildered by this enlightened Renaissance Man. Let the Renaissance begin.

▶ *Look for the following masterpieces by Leonardo 50 yards down the Grand Gallery, on the left.*

Leonardo da Vinci, The *Virgin and Child with St. Anne,* c. 1510

Three generations—grandmother, mother, and child—are arranged in a pyramid, with Anne's face as the peak and the lamb as the lower right corner. Within this balanced structure, Leonardo sets the figures in motion. Anne's legs are pointed to our left. (Is Anne *Mona?* Hmm.) Her daughter Mary, sitting on her lap, reaches to the right. Jesus looks at her playfully while turning away. The lamb pulls away from him. But even with all the twisting and turning, this is still a placid scene. It's as orderly as the geometrically perfect universe created by the Renaissance god.

There's a psychological kidney punch in this happy painting. Jesus,

Leonardo's *The Virgin and Child with St. Anne*—three generations of love

the picture of childish joy, is innocently playing with a lamb—the symbol of his inevitable sacrificial death.

The Louvre has the greatest collection of Leonardos in the world—five of them. Look for the neighboring *Virgin of the Rocks* and *John the Baptist.* Leonardo was the consummate Renaissance Man: a musician, sculptor, engineer, scientist, and sometime painter, he combined knowledge from all these areas to create beauty. If he were alive today, he'd create a Unified Field Theory in physics—and set it to music.

▶ *You'll likely find Raphael's art on the right side of the Grand Gallery, just past the statue of Diana the Huntress.*

Raphael, *La Belle Jardinière,* 1507

Raphael perfected the style Leonardo pioneered. This configuration of Madonna, Child, and John the Baptist is also a balanced pyramid with hazy grace and beauty. Mary is a mountain of maternal tenderness (the

Raphael adopted Leonardo's trademark pyramid composition for *La Belle Jardinière.*

Italian Renaissance (1400-1600)

A thousand years after Rome fell, plunging Europe into the Dark Ages, the Greek ideal of beauty was reborn in 15th-century Italy. The Renaissance—or "rebirth" of the culture of ancient Greece and Rome—was a cultural boom that changed people's thinking about every aspect of life. In politics, it meant democracy. In religion, it meant a move away from Church dominance and toward the assertion of man (humanism) and a more personal faith. Science and secular learning were revived after centuries of superstition and ignorance. In architecture, it was a return to the balanced columns and domes of Greece and Rome.

In painting, the Renaissance meant realism, and for the Italians, realism was spelled "3-D." Artists rediscovered the beauty of nature and the human body. With pictures of beautiful people in harmonious 3-D surroundings, they expressed the optimism and confidence of this new age.

title translates as "The Beautiful Gardener") as she eyes her son with a knowing look and holds his hand in a gesture of union. Jesus looks up innocently, standing *contrapposto* like a chubby Greek statue. Baby John the Baptist kneels lovingly at Jesus' feet, holding a cross that hints at his playmate's sacrificial death. The interplay of gestures and gazes gives the masterpiece both intimacy and cohesiveness, while Raphael's blended brushstrokes varnish the work with an iridescent smoothness.

With Raphael, the Greek ideal of beauty—reborn in the Renaissance—reached its peak. His work spawned so many imitators who cranked out sickly sweet, generic Madonnas that we often take him for granted. Don't. This is the real thing.

▶ *The* Mona Lisa (La Joconde) *is near the statue of Diana, in Salle 6, midway down the Grand Gallery on the right. Mona is alone behind glass on her own false wall. (You can't miss her. Just follow the signs and the people...it's the only painting you can hear. With all the groveling crowds, you can even smell it.)*

Leonardo da Vinci, *Mona Lisa,* 1503-1506

When François I invited Leonardo to France, the artist—determined to pack light—brought only a few of his paintings. One was a portrait of Lisa del Giocondo, the wife of a wealthy Florentine merchant. François immediately fell in love with the painting, making it the centerpiece of the small collection of Italian masterpieces that would, in three centuries, become the Louvre museum. He called it *La Gioconda* (*La Joconde* in French)—a play on both her last name and the Italian word for "happiness." We know it as the *Mona Lisa*—a contraction of the Italian for "my lady Lisa."

Mona may disappoint you. She's smaller than you'd expect, darker, engulfed in a huge room, and hidden behind a glaring pane of glass. So why all the hubbub? Let's take a closer look. As you would with any lover, you've got to accept her for what she is, not what you'd like her to be.

The famous smile attracts you first. Leonardo used a hazy technique called *sfumato,* blurring the edges of her mysterious smile. Try as you might, you can never quite see the corners of her mouth. Is she happy? Sad? Tender? Or is it a cynical supermodel's smirk? All visitors read it differently, projecting their own moods onto her enigmatic face. *Mona* is a Rorschach inkblot...so, how are you feeling?

Now look past the smile and the eyes that really do follow you (most eyes in portraits do) to some of the subtle Renaissance elements that make this painting work. The body is surprisingly massive and statue-like, a perfectly balanced pyramid turned at an angle, so we can see its mass. Her arm rests lightly on the armrest of a chair, almost on the level of the frame itself, as if she's sitting in a window looking out at us. The folds of her sleeves and her gently folded hands are remarkably realistic and relaxed. The typical Leonardo landscape shows distance by getting hazier and hazier.

Leonardo's *Mona Lisa*

Veronese's Venetian party scene

Though the portrait is most likely of Lisa del Giocondo, other hypotheses about the sitter's identity have been suggested, including the idea that it's Leonardo himself. Or she might be the Mama Lisa. A recent infrared scan revealed that she has a barely visible veil over her dress, which may mean (in the custom of the day) that she had just had a baby.

The overall mood is one of balance and serenity, but there's also an element of mystery. *Mona*'s smile and long-distance beauty are subtle and elusive, tempting but always just out of reach, like strands of a street singer's melody drifting through the Métro tunnel. *Mona* doesn't knock your socks off, but she winks at the patient viewer.

▶ *Before leaving* Mona, *step back and just observe the paparazzi scene. The huge canvas opposite* Mona *is...*

Paolo Veronese, *The Marriage at Cana,* 1562-1563

Stand 10 steps away from this enormous canvas to where it just fills your field of vision, and suddenly...you're in a party! Help yourself to a glass of wine. This is the Renaissance love of beautiful things gone hog-wild.

In a spacious setting of Renaissance architecture, colorful lords and ladies, decked out in their fanciest duds, feast on a great spread of food and drink, while the musicians fuel the fires of good fun. Servants prepare and serve the food, jesters play, and animals roam. In the upper left, a dog and his master look on. A sturdy linebacker in yellow pours wine out of a jug (right foreground). The man in white samples some and thinks, "Hmm, not bad," while nearby a ferocious cat battles a lion. The wedding couple at the far left is almost forgotten.

Believe it or not, this is a religious work showing the wedding celebration in which Jesus turned water into wine. And there's Jesus in the dead center of 130 frolicking figures, wondering if maybe wine coolers might not have been a better choice. With true Renaissance optimism, Venetians pictured Christ as a party animal, someone who loved the created world as much as they did.

Now, let's hear it for the band! On bass—the bad cat with the funny hat—Titian the Venetian! And joining him on viola—Crazy Veronese!

▶ *Exit behind* Mona *into the Salle Denon (Room 76). The dramatic Romantic room is to your left, and the grand Neoclassical room is to your right. Entering the Neoclassical room (Salle Daru), kneel before the largest canvas in the Louvre.*

FRENCH PAINTING (1780-1850)

Jacques-Louis David, *The Coronation of Emperor Napoleon,* **1806-1807**
Napoleon holds aloft an imperial crown. This common-born son of immigrants is about to be crowned emperor of a "New Rome." He has just made his wife, Josephine, the empress, and she kneels at his feet. Seated behind Napoleon is the pope, who journeyed from Rome to place the imperial crown on his head. But Napoleon feels that no one is worthy of the task. At the last moment, he shrugs the pope aside, grabs the crown, holds it up for all to see...and crowns himself. The pope looks p.o.'d.

After the French people decapitated their king during the Revolution (1793), their fledgling democracy floundered in chaos. France was united by a charismatic, brilliant, temperamental, upstart general who kept his feet on the ground, his eyes on the horizon, and his hand in his coat—Napoleon Bonaparte. Napoleon quickly conquered most of Europe and

Napoleon (center) crowns himself and his wife Josephine (kneeling) while the pope looks on.

insisted on being made emperor. The painter David (dah-VEED) recorded the coronation for posterity.

The radiant woman in the gallery in the background center wasn't actually there. Napoleon's mother couldn't make it to see her boy become the most powerful man in Europe, but he had David paint her in anyway. (There's a key on the frame telling who's who in the picture.) The coronation ceremony took place in Notre-Dame cathedral, which was fitted with fake columns and arches to reflect the glories of Greece and the grandeur of Rome.

David was the new emperor's official painter and propagandist, in charge of color-coordinating the costumes and flags for public ceremonies and spectacles. (Find his self-portrait with curly gray hair in the Coronation, way up in the second balcony, peeking around the tassel directly above Napoleon's crown.) As a painter, David's clean, simple style and Greek themes championed the Neoclassical style that influenced generations of artists.

▶ *As you double back toward the Romantic room, pause at Jean-Auguste-Dominique Ingres'* **La Grande Odalisque** *(1814)—a horizontal take on* Venus de Milo's *backside. Cross back through the Salle Denon and into Room 77, gushing with French Romanticism.*

Théodore Géricault, *The Raft of the Medusa,* 1819

In the artistic war between hearts and minds, the heart style was known as Romanticism. Stressing motion and emotion, it was the flip side of cool, balanced Neoclassicism, though they both flourished in the early 1800s.

What better setting for an emotional work than a shipwreck? Clinging to a raft is a tangle of bodies and lunatics sprawled over each other. The scene writhes with agitated, ominous motion—the ripple of muscles, churning clouds, and choppy seas. On the right is a deathly green corpse dangling overboard. The face of the man at left, cradling a dead body, says it all—the despair of spending weeks stranded in the middle of nowhere.

This painting was based on an actual event—150 shipwrecked people were set adrift on the open seas for 12 days, suffering hardship and hunger, even resorting to cannibalism. The story was made to order for a painter determined to shock the public—young Géricault (ZHAIR-ee-ko). He interviewed survivors and honed his craft, sketching dead bodies in the morgue and the twisted faces of lunatics in asylums, capturing the moment when all hope is lost.

Ingres' *Odalisque*—cool Neoclassicism   Géricault's *Raft*—fevered Romanticism

But wait. There's a stir in the crowd. Someone has spotted something. The bodies rise up in a pyramid of hope, culminating in a flag wave. They signal frantically, trying to catch the attention of the tiny ship on the horizon, their last desperate hope...which did finally save them. If art controls your heartbeat, this is a masterpiece.

Eugène Delacroix, *Liberty Leading the People*, 1830

The year is 1830. King Charles has just issued the 19th-century equivalent of the Patriot Act, and his subjects are angry. Parisians take to the streets once again, *Les Miz*–style, to fight royalist oppressors. The people triumph—replacing the king with Louis-Philippe, who is happy to rule within the constraints of a modern constitution. There's a hard-bitten proletarian with a sword (far left), an intellectual with a top hat and a sawed-off shotgun, and even a little boy brandishing pistols.

Leading them on through the smoke and over the dead and dying is the figure of Liberty, a strong woman waving the French flag. Does this symbol of victory look familiar? It's the *Winged Victory,* wingless and topless.

To stir our emotions, Delacroix (del-ah-kwah) uses only three major colors—the red, white, and blue of the French flag. France is the symbol of modern democracy, and this painting has long stirred its citizens' passion for liberty.

This symbol of freedom is a fitting tribute to the Louvre, the first museum ever opened to the common rabble of humanity. The good things in life don't belong only to a small, wealthy part of society, but to everyone. The motto of France is *Liberté, Egalité, Fraternité*—liberty, equality, and brotherhood for all.

Delacroix's Lady Liberty—in the classic pose of the *Winged Victory*—leads the French onward.

▶ *Exit the room at the far end (past the Café Mollien) and go downstairs, where you'll bump into the bum of a large, twisting male nude looking like he's just waking up after a thousand-year nap.*

EPILOGUE

Michelangelo, *Slaves,* 1513-1515

These two statues by earth's greatest sculptor are an appropriate end to this museum—works that bridge the ancient and modern worlds. Michelangelo, like his fellow Renaissance artists, learned from the Greeks. The perfect anatomy, twisting poses, and idealized faces appear as if they could have been created 2,000 years earlier.

The so-called *Dying Slave* (also called the *Sleeping Slave,* looking like he should be stretched out on a sofa) twists listlessly against his T-shirt-like bonds, revealing his smooth skin. Compare the polished detail of the rippling, bulging left arm with the sketchy details of the face and neck. With Michelangelo, the body does the talking. This is probably the most sensual nude Michelangelo, the master of the male body, ever created.

The *Rebellious Slave* fights against his bondage. His shoulders rotate one way, his head and leg turn the other. He looks upward, straining to get free. He even seems to be trying to free himself from the rock he's made of. Michelangelo said that his purpose was to carve away the marble to reveal the figures God put inside. This slave shows the agony of that process and the ecstasy of the result.

▶ *Tour over! These two may be slaves of the museum, but you are free to go. You've seen the essential Louvre. To leave the museum, head for the end of the hall, turn right, and follow signs down the stairs to the* Sortie.

Michelangelo's *Slaves* bridges the ancient and modern worlds.

Orsay Museum Tour

Musée d'Orsay

The Musée d'Orsay (mew-zay dor-say), housing French art from 1848-1914, picks up where the Louvre's art collection leaves off. That means Impressionism, the art of sun-dappled fields, bright colors, and crowded Parisian cafés. The Orsay houses the best general collection anywhere of Manet, Monet, Renoir, Degas, Van Gogh, Cézanne, and Gauguin. If you like Impressionism, visit this museum. If you don't like Impressionism, visit this museum. I find it a more enjoyable and rewarding place than the Louvre. Sure, ya gotta see the *Mona Lisa* and *Venus de Milo,* but after you get your gottas out of the way, enjoy the Orsay.

ORIENTATION

Cost: €11, €8.50 Tue-Wed and Fri-Sun after 16:30 and Thu after 18:00, free first Sun of month, covered by Museum Pass. Combo-tickets are available with the Orangerie (€16) or Rodin Museum (€18).

Hours: Tue-Sun 9:30-18:00, Thu until 21:45, closed Mon, last entry one hour before closing (45 minutes before on Thu). The top-floor Impressionist galleries begin closing 45 minutes early.

Free Entry near Closing Time: Right when the ticket booth stops selling tickets, visitors can often (but not always) scoot in free of charge (Tue-Wed and Fri-Sun at 17:00, Thu at 21:00; they won't let you in much after that). See the top floor first; it closes earliest.

When to Go: For shorter lines and fewer crowds, visit on Wed, Fri, or Thu evening. It's most crowded on Sun, as well as on Tue, when the Louvre is closed.

Avoiding Lines: Skip ticket-buying lines by using a Museum Pass or purchasing tickets in advance (tel. 01 40 49 48 14, www.musee-orsay. fr); both entitle you to use a separate entrance (Entrance C). Tickets and Museum Passes are sold at the newspaper kiosk just outside the Orsay entrance (along Rue de la Légion d'Honneur). If planning to get a combo-ticket with the Orangerie or Rodin, consider starting at one of those museums instead, as they have shorter lines.

Getting There: The museum is alongside the Seine River at 1 Rue de la Légion d'Honneur (Métro: Solférino, RER-C: Musée d'Orsay, bus #69, and Batobus). From the Louvre, it's a 15-minute walk through the Tuileries Garden and across the bridge. A taxi stand is in front of the entry on Quai Anatole France.

Tours: Audioguides cost €5. English guided tours usually run daily at 11:30 (€6/1.5 hours, none on Sun, tours may also run at 14:30—ask). ∩ Download my free Orsay Museum audio tour.

Length of This Tour: Allow two hours.

Cloakroom (Vestiaire): Free bag and coat check (no valuables in checked bags). Day bags (but nothing bigger) are allowed in the museum.

Photography: Photography without flash is allowed.

Cuisine Art: The snazzy $$ Le Restaurant on the second floor serves affordable tea and coffee. Less-pricey cafés are on the main floor and

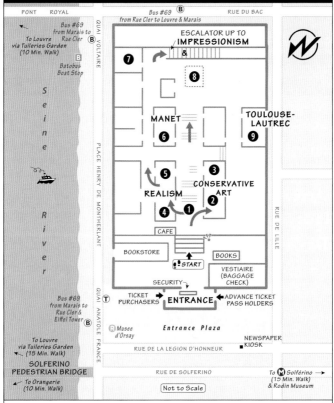

Orsay Museum—Ground Floor

PONT ROYAL

QUAI VOLTAIRE

RUE DU BAC

Bus #69
from Rue Cler to Louvre & Marais

Bus #69
from Marais to
Rue Cler
To Louvre
via Tuileries Garden
(10 Min. Walk)

B

B Batobus
Boat Step

Seine
River

PLACE HENRY DE MONTHERLANT

ESCALATOR UP TO
IMPRESSIONISM
&

❼

❽

MANET

❻

❺   ❸

REALISM

❹   ❶   ❷

**CONSERVATIVE
ART**

**TOULOUSE-
LAUTREC**

❾

RUE DE LILLE

CAFE

BOOKSTORE

❗START

BOOKS

VESTIAIRE
(BAGGAGE
CHECK)

SECURITY

QUAI ANATOLE FRANCE

Bus #69
from Marais to
Rue Cler &
Eiffel Tower
B

T TICKET
PURCHASERS

ENTRANCE

ADVANCE TICKET
PASS HOLDERS

R Musée
d'Orsay

Entrance Plaza

NEWSPAPER
■ KIOSK

To Louvre
via Tuileries Garden
← (15 Min. Walk)

RUE DE LA LEGION D'HONNEUR

SOLFERINO
PEDESTRIAN BRIDGE
← To Orangerie
(10 Min. Walk)

RUE DE SOLFERINO

Not to Scale

To M Solférino →
(15 Min. Walk)
& Rodin Museum

❶ Main Gallery Statues

❷ INGRES – The Source

❸ CABANEL – The Birth of Venus

❹ DAUMIER – Celebrities
of the Happy Medium

❺ MILLET – The Gleaners

❻ MANET – Olympia

❼ COURBET –
The Painter's Studio

❽ Opéra Exhibit

❾ TOULOUSE-LAUTREC –
Jane Avril Dancing

The Orsay's main hall—former train station

Ingres' *Source*—clean, sculptural lines

fifth floor. Outside, behind the museum, a number of classy eateries line Rue du Bac.

Starring: Manet, Monet, Renoir, Degas, Van Gogh, Cézanne, and Gauguin.

THE TOUR BEGINS

▶ *Pick up a free map and belly up to the stone balustrade overlooking the main floor.*

Trains used to run right under our feet down the center of the gallery. This former train station, the Gare d'Orsay, barely escaped the wrecking ball in the 1970s, when the French realized it'd be a great place to house the enormous collections of 19th-century art scattered throughout the city.

The ground floor (Level 0) houses early-19th-century art, mainly conservative art and Realism. On the top floor (not visible from here) is the core of the collection—the Impressionist rooms. If you're pressed for time, go directly there. We'll start with conservatives and early rebels on the ground floor, then head upstairs to see how a few visionary young artists bucked the system and revolutionized the art world, paving the way for the 20th century. Clear as Seine water? *Bien.*

Remember that the museum rotates its large collection often, so find the latest arrangement on your Orsay map, and be ready to go with the flow. (Note the location of every painting is updated daily on the website: click on "Interactive plan of the museum" at bottom of home page.)

▶ *Walk down the steps to the main floor, a gallery filled with statues.*

CONSERVATIVE ART

Main Gallery Statues

No, this isn't ancient Greece. These statues are from the same era as the Theory of Relativity. It's the conservative art of the French schools, and it was very popular for its beauty—balanced poses, perfect anatomy, sweet faces, curving lines, and gleaming white stone. (I'll bad-mouth it later, but for now appreciate the exquisite craftsmanship of this "perfect" art.)

▶ *Take your first right into the small Room 1, marked* Ingres, Delacroix, Chassériau. *Look for a nude woman with a pitcher of water.*

Ingres, *The Source (La Source)*, 1856

Let's start where the Louvre left off. Jean-Auguste-Dominique Ingres (ang-gruh), who helped cap the Louvre collection, championed a Neoclassical style. *The Source* is virtually a Greek statue on canvas. Her skin is porcelain-smooth, painted with seamless brushstrokes.

Ingres worked on this painting over the course of 35 years and considered it his "image of perfection." Famous in its day, *The Source*

The Orsay's "19th Century" (1848-1914)

Einstein and Geronimo. Abraham Lincoln and Karl Marx. The train, the bicycle, the horse and buggy, the automobile, and the balloon. Freud and Dickens. Darwin's *Origin of Species* and the Church's Immaculate Conception. Louis Pasteur and Billy the Kid. Ty Cobb and V. I. Lenin.

The 19th century was a mix of old and new, side by side. Europe was entering the modern Industrial Age, with cities, factories, rapid transit, instant communication, and global networks. At the same time, it clung to the past with traditional, rural—almost medieval—attitudes and morals.

According to the Orsay, the "19th century" began in 1848 with the socialist and democratic revolutions (Marx's *Communist Manifesto*). It ended in 1914 with the pull of an assassin's trigger, which ignited World War I and ushered in the modern world. The museum shows art that is also both old and new, conservative and revolutionary.

influenced many artists whose classical statues and paintings are in this museum.

In the Orsay's first few rooms, you're surrounded by visions of idealized beauty—nude women in languid poses, Greek mythological figures, and anatomically perfect statues. This was the art adored by French academics and the middle-class (bourgeois) public. The 19th-century art world was dominated by two conservative institutions: the Academy (the state-funded art school) and the Salon, where works were exhibited to the buying public. The art they produced was technically perfect, refined, uplifting, and heroic. Some might even say...boring.

▶ *Continue to Room 3 to find a pastel blue-green painting of a swooning Venus.*

Cabanel, *The Birth of Venus (La Naissance de Vénus)*, 1863

This painting and others nearby were popular items at the art market called the Salon. The public loved Alexandre Cabanel's *Venus*. Emperor Napoleon III purchased it.

Cabanel lays Ingres' *The Source* on her back. This goddess is a perfect fantasy, an orgasm of beauty. The Love Goddess stretches back seductively, recently birthed from the ephemeral foam of the waves. This is art of a pre-Freudian society, when sex was dirty and mysterious and had to be exalted into a more pure and divine form. French folk would literally swoon in ecstasy before these works of art.

Like it? Go ahead, swoon. If it feels good, enjoy it. (If you feel guilty, get over it.) Now, take a mental cold shower, and get ready for a Realist's view.

▶ *Cross the main gallery of statues, backtrack toward the entrance, and enter Room 4 (directly across from Ingres), marked* Daumier.

REALISM, EARLY REBELS, AND THE BELLE EPOQUE

**Daumier, *Celebrities of the Happy Medium
(Célébrités du Juste Milieu)*, 1832-1835**

This is a liberal's look at the stuffy bourgeois establishment that controlled the Academy and the Salon. In these 36 bustlets, Honoré Daumier, trained as a political cartoonist, exaggerates each subject's most distinct characteristic to capture with vicious precision the pomposity and

Cabanel's *Venus*—soft-porn fantasy

Millet's *Gleaners*—hard-core Realism

self-righteousness of these self-appointed arbiters of taste. The labels next to the busts give the name of the person being caricatured, his title or job (most were members of the French parliament), and an insulting nickname (like "gross, fat, and satisfied" or Monsieur "Platehead"). Give a few nicknames yourself. Can you find Reagan, Clinton, Kerry, Sarkozy, Al Sharpton, Gingrich, and Paul Ryan with sideburns? How about Margaret Thatcher...or is that a dude?

These people hated the art you're about to see. Their prudish faces tightened as their fantasy world was shattered by the Realists.

▶ *Nearby, find Millet's* Gleaners. *(Reminder: Paintings often move around, so you may need to use your Orsay map to find specific works.)*

Millet, *The Gleaners (Les Glaneuses),* 1867

Jean-François Millet (mee-yay) shows us three gleaners, the poor women who pick up the meager leftovers after a field has already been harvested for the wealthy. Millet grew up on a humble farm. He didn't attend the Academy and despised the uppity Paris art scene. Instead of idealized gods, goddesses, nymphs, and winged babies, he painted simple rural scenes. He was strongly affected by the socialist revolution of 1848, with its affirmation of the working class. Here he captures the innate dignity of these stocky, tanned women who bend their backs quietly in a large field for their small reward.

This is "Realism" in two senses. It's painted "realistically," not prettified. And it's the "real" world—not the fantasy world of Greek myth, but the harsh life of the working poor.

▶ *For a Realist's take on the traditional Venus, find Manet's* Olympia *in Room 14.*

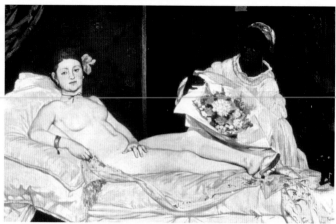

Manet's *Olympia* shocked the public, mixing a classic pose with modern frankness.

Manet, *Olympia,* 1863

"This brunette is thoroughly ugly. Her face is stupid, her skin cadaverous. All this clash of colors is stupefying." So wrote a critic when Edouard Manet's nude hung in the Salon. The public hated it, attacking Manet (man-ay) in print and literally attacking the canvas.

Compare this uncompromising nude with Cabanel's idealized, pastel, Vaseline-on-the-lens beauty in *The Birth of Venus.* Cabanel's depiction was basically soft-core pornography, the kind you see today selling lingerie and perfume.

Manet's nude doesn't gloss over anything. The pose is classic, used by Titian, Goya, and countless others. But the traditional pose is challenged by the model's jarring frankness. The sharp outlines and harsh, contrasting colors are new and shocking. Her hand is a clamp, and her stare is shockingly defiant, with not a hint of the seductive, hey-sailor look of most nudes. This prostitute, ignoring the flowers sent by her last customer, looks out as if to say, "Next." Manet replaced soft-core porn with hard-core art.

▶ *Make your way to the far left corner of level 0, to a room dominated by huge dark canvases, including...*

Courbet—behind the scenes at his studio

"Grr. I hate Impressionism."

Courbet, *The Painter's Studio (L'Atelier du Peintre)*, 1855

The Salon of 1855 rejected this dark-colored, sprawling, monumental painting that perplexed casual viewers. In an age when "Realist painter" was equated with "bomb-throwing Socialist," it took courage to buck the system. Dismissed by the so-called experts, Gustave Courbet (coor-bay) held his own one-man exhibit. He built a shed in the middle of Paris, defiantly hung his art out, and basically mooned the shocked public.

Courbet's painting takes us backstage, showing us the gritty reality behind the creation of pretty pictures. We see Courbet himself in his studio, working diligently on a Realistic landscape, oblivious to the confusion around him. Milling around are ordinary citizens, not Greek heroes. The woman who looks on is not a nude Venus but a naked artist's model. And the little boy with an adoring look on his face? Perhaps it's Courbet's inner child, admiring the artist who sticks to his guns, whether it's popular or not.

▶ At the far end of the gallery, you'll walk on a glass floor over a model of Paris.

Opéra Exhibit

Expand to 100 times your size and hover over this scale-model section of the city. In the center sits the 19th-century Opéra Garnier, with its green-domed roof. Nearby, you'll also see a cross-section model of the Opéra house and models of set designs from some famous productions. These days, Parisians enjoy their Verdi and Gounod at the modern opera house at Place de la Bastille.

The Opéra Garnier—opened in 1875—was the symbol of the belle époque, or "beautiful age." Paris was a global center of prosperity, new technology, opera, ballet, painting, and joie de vivre. But behind Paris' gilded and gas-lit exterior, a counterculture simmered.

▶ *For a taste of Parisian life during this golden age, find the Toulouse-Lautrec paintings tucked away in Room 10, to the right of the Opéra exhibit.*

Henri de Toulouse-Lautrec (1864-1901)

Henri de Toulouse-Lautrec was the black sheep of a noble family. At age 14 he broke both legs, which left him with a normal-size torso but dwarf-size limbs. Shunned by his family, a freak to society, he felt more at home in the underworld of other outcasts—prostitutes, drunks, thieves, dancers, and actors. He settled in Montmartre, where he painted the life he lived. He drank absinthe and hung out with Van Gogh. He carried a hollow cane filled with booze. When the Moulin Rouge nightclub opened, Henri was hired to do its posters. Every night, the artist put on his bowler hat and visited the Moulin Rouge to draw the crowds, the can-can dancers, and the backstage action. Toulouse-Lautrec died at age 36 of syphilis and alcoholism.

Toulouse-Lautrec's painting style captures Realist scenes with strong, curvaceous outlines. He worked quickly, creating sketches in paint that serve as snapshots of a golden era. In **Jane Avril Dancing** (**Jane Avril Dansant,** 1891), he depicts the slim, graceful, elegant, and melancholy dancer, who stood out above the rabble. Her legs keep dancing while her mind is far away. Toulouse-Lautrec, the "artistocrat," might have identified with her noble face—sad and weary of the nightlife, but immersed in it.

▶ *Next up—the Orsay's Impressionist collection. Take the escalator up to the top floor. Pause to take in a commanding view of the Orsay, pass through the bookstore, glance at the backward clock, and enter the Impressionist rooms.*

The Impressionist collection is scattered randomly through Rooms 29-36. Shadows dance and the displays mingle. Where they're hung is a lot like their brushwork...delightfully sloppy. If you don't see a described painting, just move on.

IMPRESSIONISM

Light! Color! Vibrations! You don't hang an Impressionist canvas—you

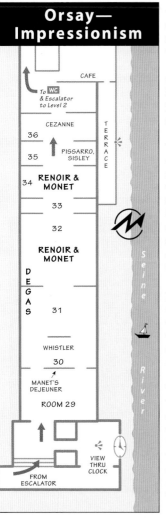

Orsay— Impressionism

CAFE

To WC
& Escalator
to Level 2

CEZANNE

36

35   PISSARRO,
SISLEY

34 **RENOIR &
MONET**

33

32

**RENOIR &
MONET**

D
E
G
A
S   31

WHISTLER

30

MANET'S
DEJEUNER

ROOM 29

FROM
ESCALATOR

VIEW
THRU
CLOCK

T
E
R
R
A
C
E

Seine River

tether it. Impressionism features bright colors, easygoing open-air scenes, spontaneity, broad brushstrokes, and the play of light.

The Impressionists made their canvases shimmer by using a simple but revolutionary technique. Let's say you mix red, yellow, and green together—you'll get brown, right? But Impressionists didn't bother to mix them. They'd slap a thick brushstroke of yellow down, then a stroke of green next to it, then red next to that. Up close, all you see are the three messy strokes, but as you back up...*voilà!* Brown! The colors blend in the eye, at a distance. But while your eye is saying, "bland old brown," your subconscious is shouting, "Red! Yellow! Green! Yes!"

There are no lines in nature, yet someone in the classical tradition (Ingres, for example) would draw an outline of his subject, then fill it in with color. Instead the Impressionists built a figure with dabs of paint...a snowman of color.

Although this top floor displays the Impressionists, you'll find a wide variety of styles. What united these artists was their commitment to everyday subjects (cafés, street scenes, landscapes, workers), their disdain for the uptight Salon, their love of color, and a sense of artistic rebellion. These painters had a love-hate relationship with the "Impressionist" label. Later in their careers, they all went their own ways and developed their own individual styles.

The Impressionists all seemed to know each other. You may see a group portrait by Henri Fantin-Latour depicting the circle of Parisian artists and intellectuals. They all learned from each other and taught each other, and they all influenced the next generation's artists (Matisse and Picasso), who created Modern art.

Remember, the following tour is less a room-by-room itinerary than an introduction to the Orsay's ever-changing collection. Have fun exploring: Think of it as a sun-dappled treasure hunt.

▶ *Start with the Impressionists' mentor, Manet, whose work is usually found in Room 29.*

Edouard Manet (1832-1883)

Manet had an upper-class upbringing and some formal art training, and

Manet, the mentor of the Impressionists, experimented with open-air painting.

Painting "in the Open Air"

The camera threatened to make artists obsolete. Now a machine could capture a better likeness faster than you could say "Etch-a-Sketch."

But true art is more than just painting reality. It gives us reality from the artist's point of view, with the artist's personal impressions of the scene. Impressions are often fleeting, so working quickly is essential.

The Impressionist painters rejected camera-like detail for a quick style more suited to capturing the passing moment. Feeling stifled by the rigid rules and stuffy atmosphere of the Academy, the Impressionists grabbed their berets and scarves and went on excursions to the country, where they set up their easels (and newly invented tubes of premixed paint) on riverbanks and hillsides, or they sketched in cafés and dance halls. Gods, goddesses, nymphs, and fantasy scenes were out; common people and rural landscapes were in.

The quick style and everyday subjects were ridiculed and called childish by the "experts." Rejected by the Salon, the Impressionists staged their own exhibition in 1874. They brashly took their name from an insult thrown at them by a critic who laughed at one of Monet's "impressions" of a sunrise. During the next decade, they exhibited their own work independently. The public, opposed at first, was slowly won over by the simplicity, color, and vibrancy of Impressionist art.

had been accepted by the Salon. He could have cranked out pretty nudes and been a successful painter, but instead he surrounded himself with a group of young artists experimenting with new techniques. His reputation and strong personality made him their master, but he also learned equally from them. Manet's thumbnail bio is typical of almost all the Impressionists: They rejected a "normal" career (lawyer, banker, grocer) to become artists, got classical art training, exhibited in the Salon, became fascinated by Realist subjects, but grew tired of the Salon's dogmatism.

Manet's **Luncheon on the Grass** (**Le Déjeuner sur l'Herbe,** 1863) shocked Paris. The staid citizens looked at this and wondered: What are these scantily clad women doing with these men? Or rather, what will they be doing after the last baguette is eaten? It isn't the nudity, but the presence of the men in ordinary clothes that suddenly makes the nudes look naked. The public judged the painting on moral rather than artistic terms.

You can see that a new revolutionary movement was starting to bud—Impressionism. Notice the background: the messy brushwork of trees and leaves, the play of light on the pond, and the light that filters through the trees onto the woman who stoops in the haze. Also note the strong contrast of colors (white skin, black clothes, green grass). This is a true out-of-doors painting, not a studio production.

Let the Impressionist revolution begin!

Edgar Degas (1834-1917)

Degas (day-gah) was a rich kid from a family of bankers, and he got the best classical-style art training. He painted in the Academic style, exhibited in the Salon, gained a good reputation, and then...he met the Impressionists.

Degas blends classical lines and Realist subjects with Impressionist color, spontaneity, and everyday scenes from urban Paris. He loved the unposed "snapshot" effect, catching his models off guard. Dance students, women at work, and café scenes are approached from odd angles that aren't always ideal but make the scenes seem more real. He gives us the backstage view of life.

Degas loved dance and the theater. The play of stage lights off his dancers, especially the halos of ballet skirts, is made to order for an Impressionist. A dance rehearsal let Degas capture a behind-the-scenes look at bored, tired, restless dancers (***The Dance Class, La Classe de Danse,*** c. 1873-1875). Besides his oil paintings of dancers, you may also

A favorite Monet subject—the Japanese Bridge at Giverny

Degas—a behind-the-scenes look at dancers

Degas took "snapshots" of ordinary people—at work, at the theater, or in a late-night café.

see his small statues of them—he first modeled the figures in wax, then cast them in bronze.

Degas hung out with low-life Impressionists, discussing art, love, and life in the cheap cafés and bars in Montmartre. In the painting **In a Café** (**Dans un Café,** 1875-1876), a weary lady of the evening meets morning with a last, lonely, nail-in-the-coffin drink in the glaring light of a four-in-the-morning café. The pale green drink at the center of the composition is the toxic substance absinthe, which fueled many artists and burned out many more.

▶ *Scattered all around you are works by two Impressionist masters at their peak, Monet and Renoir. You're looking at the quintessence of Impressionism. The two were good friends, often working side by side, and their canvases sometimes hang side by side in these rooms.*

Claude Monet (1840-1926)
Monet (mo-nay) is the father of Impressionism. He fully explored the possibilities of open-air painting and tried to faithfully reproduce nature's colors

with bright blobs of paint. Throughout his long career, more than any of his colleagues, Monet stuck to the Impressionist credo of creating objective studies in color and light.

In the 1860s, Monet (along with Renoir) began painting landscapes in the open air. Although Monet did the occasional urban scene, he was most at home in the countryside, painting farms, rivers, trees, and passing clouds. He studied optics and pigments to know just the right colors he needed to reproduce the shimmering quality of reflected light. The key was to work quickly—at that "golden hour" (to use a modern photographer's term), when the light was just right. Then he'd create a fleeting "impression" of the scene.

Monet is known for his series of paintings on the same subject. For example, you may see several canvases of the cathedral in Rouen. In 1893, Monet went to Rouen, rented a room across from the cathedral, set up his easel...and waited. He wanted to catch "a series of differing impressions" of the cathedral facade at various times of day and year. He often had several canvases going at once. In all, he did 30 paintings of the cathedral, and each is unique. The time-lapse series shows the sun passing slowly across the sky, creating different-colored light and shadows. The labels next to the art describe the conditions: in gray weather, in the morning, morning sun, full sunlight, and so on.

As Monet zeroed in on the play of colors and light, the physical subject—the cathedral—dissolved. It's only a rack upon which to hang the light and color. Later artists would boldly throw away the rack, leaving purely abstract modern art in its place.

One of Monet's favorite places to paint was the garden he landscaped at his home in Giverny, west of Paris (and worth a visit, provided you like Monet more than you hate crowds). The Japanese bridge and the water lilies floating in the pond were his two favorite subjects. As Monet aged and his eyesight failed, he made bigger canvases of smaller subjects. The final water lilies (at the Orangerie and Marmottan museums) are monumental smudges of thick paint surrounded by paint-splotched clouds that are reflected on the surface of the pond.

Pierre-Auguste Renoir (1841-1919)

Renoir (ren-wah) started out as a painter of landscapes, along with Monet, but later veered from the Impressionist's philosophy and painted images that were unabashedly "pretty." He populated his canvases with

Monet's cathedral dissolves into a pattern of paint, pointing the way toward purely abstract art.

rosy-cheeked, middle-class girls performing happy domestic activities, rendered in a warm, inviting style. As Renoir himself said, "There are enough ugly things in life."

Renoir's lighthearted work uses light colors—no brown or black. The paint is thin and translucent, and the outlines are soft, so the figures blend seamlessly with the background. He seems to be searching for an ideal, the sort of pure beauty we saw in paintings on the ground floor.

In his last years (when he was confined to a wheelchair with arthritis), Renoir turned to full-figured nudes—like those painted by Old Masters such as Rubens or Boucher. He introduced more and more red tones, as if trying for even greater warmth.

Renoir's best-known work is **Dance at the Moulin de la Galette** (**Bal du Moulin de la Galette,** 1876). On Sunday afternoons, working-class folk would dress up and head for the fields on Butte Montmartre (near Sacré-Cœur basilica) to dance, drink, and eat little crêpes *(galettes)*

Renoir—in this scene from Montmartre—captures the joie de vivre of the belle époque.

till dark. Renoir liked to go there to paint the common Parisians living and loving in the afternoon sun. The sunlight filtering through the trees creates a kaleidoscope of colors, like the 19th-century equivalent of a mirror ball throwing darts of light onto the dancers.

He captured the dappled light with quick blobs of yellow staining the ground, the men's jackets, and the sun-dappled straw hat (right of center). Smell the powder on the ladies' faces. The painting glows with bright colors. Even the shadows on the ground, which should be gray or black, are colored a warm blue. Like a photographer who uses a slow shutter speed to show motion, Renoir paints a waltzing blur.

▸ *Before moving on, check out some of the "lesser" pioneers of the Impressionist style—Pissarro, Sisley, and others.*

Paul Cézanne (1839-1906)

Cézanne (say-zahn) brought Impressionism into the 20th century. After the color of Monet and the warmth of Renoir, Cézanne's rather impersonal canvases can be difficult to appreciate. Bowls of fruit, landscapes, and a few portraits were Cézanne's passion (see **The Card Players, Les Joueurs de Cartes,** 1890-1895). Because of his style (not the content), he is often called the first modern painter.

Cézanne was virtually unknown and unappreciated in his lifetime. He worked alone, lived alone, and died alone, ignored by all but a few revolutionary young artists who understood his genius.

Unlike the Impressionists, who painted what they saw, Cézanne reworked reality. He simplified it into basic geometric forms—circular apples, rectangular boulders, cone-shaped trees, triangular groups of people. He might depict a scene from multiple angles—showing a tabletop from above but the bowl of fruit resting on it from the side. He laid paint with heavy brushstrokes, blending the background and foreground to obliterate traditional 3-D depth. He worked slowly, methodically, stroke by stroke—a single canvas could take months.

Where the Impressionists built a figure out of a mosaic of individual brushstrokes, Cézanne used blocks of paint to create a more solid, geometrical shape. These chunks are like little "cubes." It's no coincidence that his experiments in reducing forms to their geometric basics inspired the...Cubists.

▸ *Break time. Continue to the jazzy café, which serves small-plate fare*

Cézanne built this scene out of patches of paint, anticipating the "cubes" of Cubism.

with savoir faire. Or venture out on the terrace for fresh air and great views.

You'll find the Post-Impressionists downstairs. To get there from the café, find the down escalators and descend to level 2. Go along the right side of the open-air mezzanine, where you'll find the entrance to Rooms 71-72, containing works by Van Gogh and Gauguin mixed together.

POST-IMPRESSIONISM

Post-Impressionism—the style that employs Impressionism's bright colors while branching out in new directions—is scattered all around the museum. We got a taste of the style with Paul Cézanne, and it continues here on level 2 with…

Level 2—Post-Impressionism & Beyond

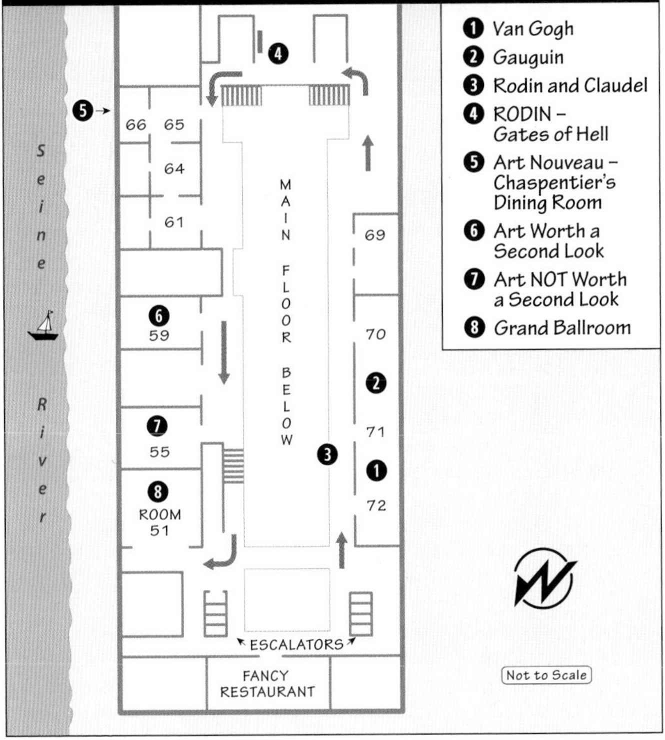

❶ Van Gogh
❷ Gauguin
❸ Rodin and Claudel
❹ RODIN – Gates of Hell
❺ Art Nouveau – Chaspentier's Dining Room
❻ Art Worth a Second Look
❼ Art NOT Worth a Second Look
❽ Grand Ballroom
Seine River
66
65
64
61
59
55
ROOM 51
69
70
71
72
MAIN FLOOR BELOW
ESCALATORS
FANCY RESTAURANT
Not to Scale

Vincent van Gogh (1853-1890)

Impressionists have been accused of being "light"-weights. The colorful style lends itself to bright country scenes, gardens, sunlight on the water, and happy crowds of simple people. It took a remarkable genius to add profound emotion to the Impressionist style.

Like Michelangelo, Beethoven, and a select handful of others, Vincent van Gogh (pronounced van-go, or van-HOCK by the Dutch and the snooty)

Van Gogh's Room at Arles

put so much of himself into his work that art and life became one. In the Orsay's collection of paintings, you'll see both Van Gogh's painting style and his life unfold.

Vincent was the son of a Dutch minister. He too felt a religious calling, and he spread the gospel among the poorest of the poor—peasants and miners in overcast Holland and Belgium. He painted these hardworking, dignified folks in a crude, dark style reflecting the oppressiveness of their lives...and his own loneliness as he roamed northern Europe in search of a calling.

Encouraged by his art-dealer brother, Van Gogh moved to Paris, and *voilà!* The color! He met Monet, drank with Gauguin and Toulouse-Lautrec, and soaked up the Impressionist style. (For example, see how he might build a bristling brown beard using thick strokes of red, yellow, and green side by side.)

At first, he painted like the others, but soon he developed his own style. By using thick, swirling brushstrokes, he infused life into even inanimate objects. Van Gogh's brushstrokes curve and thrash like a garden hose pumped with wine.

The social life of Paris became too much for the solitary Van Gogh, and he moved to the south of France. At first, in the glow of the bright spring sunshine, he had a period of incredible creativity and happiness. He was overwhelmed by the bright colors, landscape vistas, and common people. It was an Impressionist's dream (see **Midday, La Méridienne,** 1889-90). But being alone in a strange country began to wear on him. An ugly man, he found it hard to get a date. A painting of his rented bedroom in Arles shows a cramped, bare-bones place (**Van Gogh's Room at Arles, La Chambre de Van Gogh à Arles,** 1889). He invited his friend Gauguin to join him, but after two months together arguing passionately about art, nerves got raw. Van Gogh threatened Gauguin with a razor, which drove his friend back to Paris. In crazed despair, Van Gogh cut off a piece of his own ear.

The people of Arles realized they had a madman on their hands and

Van Gogh's *Midday, La Méridienne*—painted during a happy time in the south of France

In Van Gogh's *Self-Portrait,* the swirl of brushstrokes captures the artist's restless energy.

convinced Vincent to seek help at a mental hospital. The paintings he finished in the peace of the hospital are more meditative—there are fewer bright landscapes and more closed-in scenes with deeper, almost surreal colors. Van Gogh, the preacher's son, saw painting as a calling, and he approached it with a spiritual intensity. In his last days, he wavered between happiness and madness. He despaired of ever being sane enough to continue painting.

His final self-portrait shows a man engulfed in a confused background of brushstrokes that swirl and rave (**Self-Portrait, Portrait de l'Artiste,** 1889). But in the midst of this rippling sea of mystery floats a still, detached island of a face. Perhaps his troubled eyes know that in only a few months, he'll take a pistol and put a bullet through his chest.

▶ *Also in Rooms 71-72, look for...*

Paul Gauguin (1848-1903)

Gauguin (go-gan) got the travel bug early in childhood and grew up wanting to be a sailor. Instead, he became a stockbroker. In his spare time, he painted, and he was introduced to the Impressionist circle. He learned their bright clashing colors but diverged from their path about the time Van Gogh waved a knife in his face. At the age of 35, he got fed up with it all, quit his job, abandoned his wife (her stern portrait bust may be nearby) and family, and took refuge in his art.

Gauguin traveled to the South Seas in search of the exotic, finally settling on Tahiti. There he found his Garden of Eden. He simplified his life into a routine of eating, sleeping, and painting. He simplified his paintings still more, to flat images with heavy black outlines filled with bright, pure colors. The background and foreground colors are equally bright, producing a flat, stained-glass-like surface.

Gauguin's best-known works capture an idyllic Tahitian landscape

Gauguin paints his primitive paradise, using childlike blocks of bright color.

Rodin worked in bronze, so there are authorized versions of this work elsewhere.

peopled by exotic women engaged in simple tasks and making music (**Arearea,** 1892). The native girls lounge placidly in unselfconscious innocence (so different from Cabanel's seductive, melodramatic *Venus*). The style is intentionally "primitive," collapsing the three-dimensional landscape into a two-dimensional pattern of bright colors. Gauguin intended that this simple style carry a deep undercurrent of symbolic meaning. He wanted to communicate to his "civilized" colleagues back home that he'd found the paradise he'd always envisioned.

▶ *Stroll the statue-lined open-air mezzanine from the near end (near room 72) to the far end, enjoying the work of Rodin, Claudel, and other greats of...*

FRENCH SCULPTURE

Auguste Rodin (1840-1917)

Born of working-class roots and largely self-taught, Rodin (ro-dan) combined classical solidity with Impressionist surfaces to become the greatest sculptor since Michelangelo. He labored in obscurity for decades, making knickknacks and doorknobs for a construction company. By age 40, he started to gain recognition. He became romantically involved with a student, Camille Claudel, who became his model and muse.

Rodin's subject was always the human body, showing it in unusual poses that express inner emotion. The surface is alive, rippling with frosting-like gouges.

The style comes from Rodin's work process. Rodin paid models to run, squat, leap, and spin around his studio however they wanted. When he saw an interesting pose, he'd yell, "Freeze!" (or "statue maker") and get out his sketchpad. Rodin worked quickly, using his powerful thumbs to make a small statue in clay, which he would then reproduce as a life-size clay statue that in turn was used as a mold for casting a plaster or bronze copy. Authorized copies of Rodin's work are now included in museums all over the world.

Like his statue **The Walking Man** (**L'Homme Qui Marche,** c. 1900), Rodin had one foot in the past, while the other stepped into the future. This muscular, forcefully striding man could be a symbol of Renaissance Man with his classical power. With no mouth or hands, he speaks with his body. But get close and look at the statue's surface. This rough, "unfinished" look reflects light in the same way the rough Impressionist brushwork does, making the statue come alive, never quite at rest in the viewer's eye.

Camille Claudel (1864-1943)

Claudel was Rodin's student and mistress. In **Maturity (*L'Age Mur,*** 1899-1903)—a small bronze statue group of three figures—Claudel may have portrayed their doomed love affair. A young girl desperately reaches out to an older man, who is led away reluctantly by an older woman. The center of the composition is the empty space left when their hands separate. In real life, Rodin refused to leave his wife, and Claudel ended up in an insane asylum.

▶ *Continue along the mezzanine to the far end, where you'll find another well-known work by Rodin.*

Rodin, *The Gates of Hell (La Porte de l'Enfer),* 1880-1917

Rodin worked for decades on these doors depicting Dante's hell, and they contain some of his greatest hits—small statues that he later executed in full size. Find *The Thinker* squatting above the doorway, contemplating Man's fate. The doors' 186 figures eventually inspired larger versions of *The Kiss,* the *Three Shades,* and more.

From this perch in the Orsay, look down to the main floor at all the classical statues between you and the big clock, and realize how far we've come—not in years, but in stylistic changes. Many of the statues below—beautiful, smooth, balanced, and idealized—were created at the same time as Rodin's powerful, haunting works. Rodin's sculptures capture the groundbreaking spirit of much of the art in the Orsay Museum. With a stable base of 19th-century stone, he launched art into the 20th century.

Claudel was dumped by Rodin.   Salle des Fêtes (Grand Ballroom)

▶ You've seen the essential Orsay and are permitted to cut out. But if you have extra time, there's an "other" Orsay you may find entertaining. The beauty of the Orsay is that it combines all the art from 1848 to 1914, both modern and classical, in one building. Rooms 61-66 are a curvaceous IKEA of Art Nouveau furniture. Rooms 55 and 59 feature some non-Impressionist art—so popular in the 19th century and now so unpopular. The chandeliered Salle des Fêtes (Grand Ballroom, Room 51) was once one of Paris' poshest nightspots.

Is this stuff beautiful or merely gaudy? Divine or decadent? Whatever you decide, it was all part of the marvelous world of the Orsay's century of art.

One last look—at the main floor, the mezzanine, and the great art we've seen on this tour

Eiffel Tower Tour

La Tour Eiffel

It's crowded, expensive, and there are probably better views in Paris, but visiting this 1,000-foot-tall ornament is worth the trouble. Visitors to Paris may find *Mona Lisa* to be less than expected, but the Eiffel Tower rarely disappoints, even in an era of skyscrapers. This is a once-in-a-lifetime, I've-been-there experience. Making the eye-popping ascent and ear-popping descent gives you membership in the exclusive society of the quarter of a billion other humans who have made the Eiffel Tower the most visited monument in the modern world.

ORIENTATION

Cost: €25 to the top; €16 to the two lower levels or €10 to climb the stairs to the lower levels (must buy summit elevator before entering tower), less if you're under 25, not covered by Museum Pass.

Hours: Daily 9:00-24:45, Sept-mid-June 9:30-23:45; last ascent to top at 22:30 and to lower levels at 23:00 all year (elevator and stairs). Top level can close temporarily in windy weather or when it reaches capacity.

Buying Tickets in Advance: It's strongly advised to book a reservation online. At www.toureiffel.paris, you can book an entry time and skip the initial entry line (the longest) at no extra cost. Online ticket sales open up about three months before any given date (at 8:30 Paris time)—and can sell out within hours (especially for April-Sept). If no slots are available, try buying a "Lift entrance ticket with access to 2nd floor." Or, try the website again a week before your visit—last-minute spots may open up. A security fence/glass wall rings the base of the tower with one access point at each side, so allow an extra 30 minutes to go through security before your appointed time.

Without a reservation, get in line 30 minutes before the tower opens or go later in the day (after 19:00 May-Aug, after 17:00 off-season), or take the (less-crowded) stairs. To avoid lines for the elevator to the top level, you could just enjoy the fine views from the second level. A reservation at either of the tower's restaurants lets you skip the worst lines (see "Eating," later). Fat Tire Tours sells guided tours (€46-64) that get you to the second level or the tower's summit.

When to Go: For the best of all worlds, arrive with enough light to see the views, then stay as it gets dark to see the lights.

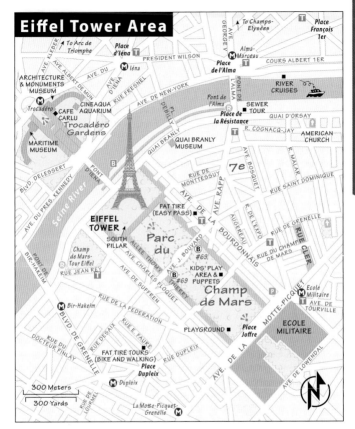

Getting There: The Bir-Hakeim and Trocadéro Métro stops, and the Champ de Mars-Tour Eiffel RER stop, are each about a 10-minute walk away. The Ecole Militaire Métro stop in the Rue Cler area is 20 minutes away. Buses #42, #69, and #87 stop nearby.

Information: Information offices are between the north and east pillars and at the west pillar, next to the Group Desk. Recorded info tel. 08 92 70 12 39, www.toureiffel.paris.

Eiffel Tower

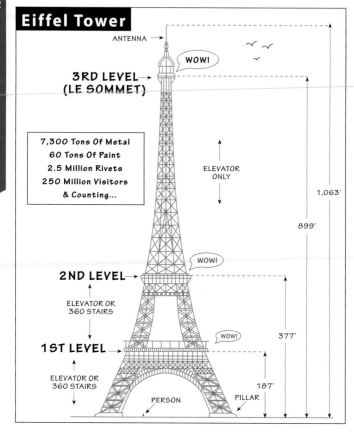

ANTENNA →

WOW!

3RD LEVEL →
(LE SOMMET)

7,300 Tons Of Metal
60 Tons Of Paint
2.5 Million Rivets
250 Million Visitors
& Counting...

ELEVATOR
ONLY

1,063'

899'

WOW!

2ND LEVEL →

ELEVATOR OR
360 STAIRS

WOW!

1ST LEVEL →

377'

ELEVATOR OR
360 STAIRS

187'

PERSON

PILLAR

Length of This Tour: With a reservation and minimal crowds, figure 90
minutes to the top and back. It takes three to four hours with crowds
and lines.

Pickpockets: In crowded elevators and lines, *en garde.*

Security Check: Bags larger than 19" × 8" × 12" are not allowed, and there is no baggage check. All bags are subject to a security search. No knives, glass bottles, or cans are permitted.

Services: Free WCs are at the base of the tower behind the east pillar. Inside the tower, WCs are on all levels, but they have long lines.

Photography: No restrictions.

Eating: The first and second levels have small sandwich-and-pizza-type ca-fés, and the first level occasionally has temporary "pop-up" restaurants.

The tower's two classy $$$$ restaurants offer great views, and a reservation at either restaurant lets you skip the initial elevator line. Reserve far in advance for a view table, especially at dinner. On the first level is 58 Tour Eiffel (€42 lunches; €85-185 dinners, open daily, tel. 01 72 76 18 46, www.restaurants-toureiffel.com). The more ex-pensive Jules Verne Restaurant is on the second level (€105 weekday lunch *menu*, €190-230 weekend lunch or daily dinner *menus*, tel. 01 45 55 61 44, www.lejulesverne-paris.com).

At the tower's base, there's not much besides sandwich stands. Rue Cler, with many options, is a 20-minute walk away (✪ see pages 188–189). Avenue de la Bourdonnais, a block east of the tower, has a few eateries and sandwich shops. The nearby $$ Quai Branly Museum garden café is good but relatively pricey.

Your tastiest option may be to assemble a picnic beforehand to eat alongside the Champ de Mars park. The center of the park is off-limits to picnickers.

Starring: All of Paris...and beyond.

THE TOUR BEGINS

There are three observation platforms, at 200, 400, and 900 feet. Although being on the windy top of the Eiffel Tower is a thrill you'll never forget, the view is better from the second level, where you can actually see Paris' monuments. All three levels have some displays, WCs, souvenir stores, and a few other services.

For the hardy, stairs lead from the ground level up to the first level (360 steps) and second level (another 360 steps). The staircase is enclosed with a wire cage, so you can't fall, but those with vertigo issues may still find them dizzying.

If you want to see the entire tower, from top to bottom, then see it...

Up and Down

The tower—which was de-signed from the start to accom-modate hordes of visitors—has always had elevators. Back in the late 19th century, elevator technology was so new that they needed a special design to accommodate the angle of the tower's pillars. Today's elevators (modern replacements) make about 100 round-trip journeys a day.

There are 1,665 stairs up to the top level, though tourists can only climb 720 of them, up as far as the second level. During a race in 1905, a gentleman climbed from the ground to the second floor—elevation gain 400 feet—in 3 minutes, 12 seconds.

from top to bottom. Ride the elevator to the second level (if your elevator stops at the first level on the way up, don't get off), then immediately line up for the next elevator to the top. Enjoy the views, then ride back down to the second level. Frolic there for a while, then descend to the first level via the stairs (no line) or elevator (ask if it will stop on the first level—some don't). After more views, shops, exhibits, and a snack, take the elevator or stairs back down to earth.

▶ *Find the various entrances at the base of the tower's four* piliers *(pillars), named for their compass points:* nord, sud, est, *and* ouest. *Make sure you get in the right line. If you have a reservation, look for signs saying* Visiteurs avec Reservation *(Visitors with Reservation). Otherwise, follow signs for* Individuels *or* Visiteurs sans Tickets *(avoid lines selling tickets only for* Groupes*). To climb the stairs, enter at the south pillar, next to* Le Jules Verne *restaurant entrance. As you wait to enter, gaze up at the tower towering above you, and don't even think about what would hap-pen if someone dropped a coin from the top.*

Eiffel—designer, financier, and builder

Wheels turn cables to lift the elevator.

Exterior

Delicate and graceful when seen from afar, the Eiffel Tower is massive—even a bit scary—close up. You don't appreciate its size until you walk toward it; like a mountain, it seems so close but takes forever to reach.

The tower, including its antenna, stands 1,063 feet tall, or slightly higher than the 77-story Chrysler Building in New York. Its four support pillars straddle an area of 3.5 acres. Despite the tower's 7,300 tons of metal and 60 tons of paint, it is so well-engineered that it weighs no more per square inch at its base than a linebacker on tiptoes.

Once the world's tallest structure, it's now eclipsed by a number of towers (Tokyo Skytree, 2,080 feet, for one), radio antennae (KVLY-TV Mast, North Dakota, 2,063 feet), and skyscrapers (the Burj Khalifa in Dubai, UAE, 2,717 feet).

The long green lawn stretching south of the tower is the Champ de Mars, originally the training ground for troops and students of the nearby Military School (Ecole Militaire) and now a park. On the north side, across the Seine, is the curved palace colonnade framing a square called the Trocadéro.

History

The first visitor to the Paris World's Fair in 1889 walked beneath the "arch" formed by the newly built Eiffel Tower and entered the fairgrounds. This event celebrated both the centennial of the French Revolution and France's position as a global superpower. Bridge builder Gustave Eiffel (1832-1923) won the contest to build the fair's centerpiece by beating out such rival proposals as a giant guillotine.

Eiffel deserved to have the tower named for him. He not only designed

Building the Tower

As you ascend through the metal beams, imagine being a worker, perched high above nothing, riveting this thing together. It was a massive project, and it took all the ingenuity of the Industrial Age—including mass production, cutting-edge technology, and capitalist funding.

An 18,000-piece Erector set

The tower went up like an 18,000-piece erector set, made of 15-foot iron beams held together with 2.5 million rivets. For two years, 300 workers assembled the pieces, the tower rising as they went.

First, they sank massive iron pillars into the ground at an angle, surrounded by cement 20 feet thick and capped with stone. They erected wooden scaffolding to support the lower (angled) sections,

it, he financed it, his factory produced the iron beams, he invented special cranes and apparatus, and—working on a deadline for the World's Fair—he brought in the project on time and under budget.

The tower was nothing but a showpiece, with no functional purpose except to demonstrate to the world that France had the wealth, knowledge, and can-do spirit to erect a structure far taller than anything the world had ever seen. The original plan was to dismantle the tower as quickly as it was built after the celebration ended, but it was kept by popular demand.

To a generation hooked on technology, the tower was the marvel of the age, a symbol of progress and human ingenuity. Not all were so impressed, however; many found it a monstrosity. The writer Guy de Maupassant (1850-1893) routinely ate lunch in the tower just so he wouldn't have to look at it.

In subsequent years, the tower has come to serve many functions: as a radio transmitter (1909-present), a cosmic-ray observatory (1910), a until the pillars came together and the tower could support itself. Then the iron beams were lifted up with steam-powered cranes, including some on tracks (creeper cranes) that inched up the pillars as the tower progressed. There, daring workers dangled from rope ladders, balanced on beams, and tightrope-walked their way across them as they put the pieces in place. The workers then hammered in red-hot rivets that, as they cooled, locked the structure in place.

After a mere year and a half, the tower surpassed what had been the tallest structure in the world—the Washington Monument (555 feet)—which had taken 36 years to build.

The tower was painted a rusty red. Since then, it's sported several colors, including mustard and the current brown-gray. It is repainted every seven years, a process that takes 25 full-time painters 18 months to apply 60 tons of paint by hand—no spraying allowed.

Two years, two months, and five days after construction began, the tower was done. On May 15, 1889, a red, white, and blue beacon was lit on the top, the World's Fair began, and the tower carried its first astounded visitor to the top.

billboard (spelling "Citroën" in lights, 1925-1934), a broadcaster of Nazi TV programs (1940-1944), a fireworks launch pad (numerous times), and as a framework for dazzling lighting displays, including the current arrangement, designed in 2000 for the celebration of the millennium.

▶ *To reach the top, ride the elevator or walk to the second level. From there, get in line for the next elevator and continue to the top. Pop out 900 feet above the ground.*

Third Level (*Le Sommet,* or Summit)

You'll find wind and grand, sweeping views on the tiny top level. The city lies before you, with a panorama guide. On a good day, you can see for 40 miles. Do a 360-degree tour of Paris.

Looking west *(ouest)*: The Seine runs east to west (though at this point it's flowing more southwest). At the far end of the skinny "island" in the river, find the tiny copy of the Statue of Liberty, looking 3,633 miles

Looking west—next stop, New York   Looking north—Place du Trocadéro

away to her big sister in New York. Gustave Eiffel, a man of many talents, also designed the internal supports of New York's Statue of Liberty, which was cast in copper by fellow Frenchman Frederic Bartholdi (1886).

Looking north *(nord)*: At your feet is the curved arcade of the Trocadéro, itself the site of a World's Fair in 1878. Beyond that is the vast, forested expanse of the Bois de Boulogne, the three-square-mile park that hosts joggers and *boules* players by day and prostitutes by night. In the far distance are the skyscrapers of La Défense, and to the right of the Trocadéro is the Arc de Triomphe.

Looking east *(est)*: At your feet are the Seine and its many bridges, including the Pont Alexandre, with its four golden statues. Looking farther upstream, find the Orsay Museum, the Louvre, Pont Neuf, and the twin towers of Notre-Dame.

On the Right Bank (to your left) is the bullet-shaped dome of Sacré-Cœur, atop Butte Montmartre.

Looking south *(sud)*: In a line, find the Champ de Mars, the Ecole Militaire, the Y-shaped UNESCO building, and the 689-foot Montparnasse Tower skyscraper. To the left is the golden dome of Les Invalides.

The Tippy Top: Ascend another short staircase to the open-air top, beneath satellite dishes. You'll see the tiny apartment given to Gustave Eiffel. The mannequins re-create the moment during the 1889 World's Fair when the American Thomas Edison paid a visit to his fellow techie, Gustave (the one with the beard) and Gustave's daughter Claire, presenting them with his new invention, a phonograph. (Then they cranked it up and blasted The Who's "I Can See for Miles.")

▶ *Ride the elevator down to the...*

Second Level

The second level (400 feet) has the best views because you're closer to the sights, and the monuments are more recognizable. This level has souvenir shops, WCs, and a small stand-up café.

The world-class Le Jules Verne restaurant on this level is currently run by celebrity chef Alain Ducasse. One would hope his brand of haute cuisine matches the 400-foot haute of the restaurant.

▶ *Catch the elevator or take the stairs (5 minutes, 360 steps, free) down to the...*

First Level

The first level (200 feet) has more great views, all well-described by the tower's panoramic displays. After a $38 million renovation, this level is decked out with new shops, eateries, and displays, as well as a private reception hall. Pop-up restaurants and kiosks appear with every season— even a little playground for kids. In winter, part of the first level is often set up to host an ice-skating rink.

The highlight is the glass floor—venture onto it to experience what it's like to stand atop an 18-story building and look straight down.

The 58 Tour Eiffel restaurant has more accessible prices than Le Jules Verne restaurant above, and is also run by Alain Ducasse.

Watch the original hydraulic pump (1889) at work. It once pumped water from here to the second level to feed the machinery powering the upper elevator. Then look at the big wheels that wind and unwind heavy cables to lift the elevators.

Explore the various exhibits. You might learn how the sun warms the tower's metal, causing the top to expand and lean about five inches away from the sun, or how the tower oscillates slightly in the wind. Because of its lacy design, even the strongest of winds can't blow the tower down, but only cause it to sway a few inches. Eiffel designed the tower primarily with wind resistance in mind, wanting a structure seemingly "molded by the action of the wind itself."

▶ *Consider a drink or a sandwich while overlooking all of Paris, then take the elevator or stairs (5 minutes, 360 steps) to the ground.*

The Tour Ends

Welcome back to earth.

For a final look, stroll to Place du Trocadéro or to the end of the Champ de Mars and look back for great views. However impressive it may be by day, the tower is an awesome thing to see at twilight, when it becomes engorged with light, and virile Paris lies back and lets night be on top. When darkness fully envelops the city, the tower seems to climax with a spectacular light show at the top of each hour...for five minutes.

The tower is lit from within. At the top of the hour, it sparkles and projects a beacon of light.

Rue Cler Walk

The Art of Parisian Living

A stroll down this open-air-market street introduces you to a thriving, traditional Parisian neighborhood and its local culture. And although Rue Cler is a wealthy and quickly changing district, it retains the everyday charm still found in most neighborhoods throughout the city.

In food-crazy Paris, shopping for groceries is the backbone of daily life. Rue Cler, traffic-free since 1984, is lined with the essential shops— wine, cheese, bread, and chocolate. To learn the fine art of living Parisian-style, there's no better classroom than Rue Cler. Explore the shops and assemble the ultimate French picnic.

THE WALK BEGINS

▶ *Start your walk at the northern end of the pedestrian section of Rue Cler, at Rue de Grenelle (right by a bus #69 stop and a short walk from Mo: Ecole Militaire). Visit Rue Cler when its markets are open and lively (Tue-Sat 8:30-13:00 or 15:00-19:30, Sun 8:30-12:00, dead on Mon). Allow an hour to browse and café-hop along this short, three-block walk.*

❶ Café Roussillon

This café is a neighborhood fixture. To the left of the door, you'll see the *Tarif des Consommations* sign required by French law, making the pricing clear: Drinks served at the bar *(comptoir)* are cheaper than drinks served at the tables *(salles)*. Inside, the bar is always busy. The blackboard lists wines sold by the little, 7-centiliter glass (about 2.5 ounces), along with other drinks.

The small **late-night grocery** next door is one of many neighborhood shops nicknamed *dépanneurs* ("to help you out of difficulty"). Open nightly until midnight, these Parisian 7-Elevens are usually run by hardworking North Africans willing to keep long hours. Locals happily pay the higher prices for the convenience *dépanneurs* provide.

▶ *If you're shopping for designer baby clothes, you'll find them across the street at...*

❷ Petit Bateau

The French spend at least as much on their babies as they do on their dogs—dolling them up with designer jammies. This store is one in a popular chain. Babies-in-the-know just aren't comfortable unless they're making a fashion statement (such as underwear with sailor stripes). Whereas much of Europe faces an aging and shrinking population, France is having a baby boom—an average of two children per family, compared with 1.6 for the rest of Europe. Babies are trendy, and the government rewards parents with big tax incentives for their first two children—and then doubles the incentive after that.

▶ *Cross Rue de Grenelle to find...*

❸ Top Halles Fruits and Vegetables

Each morning, fresh produce is trucked in from farmers' fields to Paris' huge Rungis market—Europe's largest, near Orly Airport—and then

Rue Cler Walk

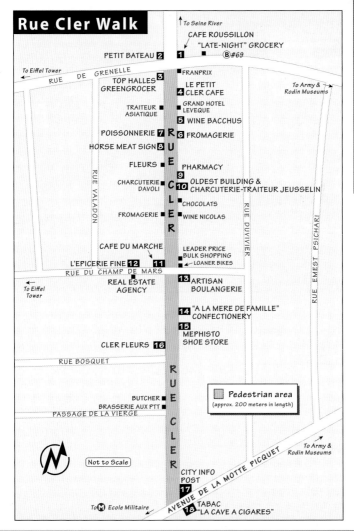

↑ To Seine River

CAFE ROUSSILLON
"LATE-NIGHT" GROCERY
■ **B**#69

■ **1**

PETIT BATEAU **2**

To Eiffel Tower ←
RUE DE GRENELLE

■ FRANPRIX

TOP HALLES **3**
GREENGROCER

LE PETIT
4 CLER CAFE

To Army & →
Rodin Museums

TRAITEUR ■
ASIATIQUE

■ GRAND HOTEL
LEVEQUE

5 WINE BACCHUS

POISSONNERIE **7** **R** **6** FROMAGERIE

HORSE MEAT SIGN **8** **U**

E

FLEURS ■ PHARMACY

C **9**

CHARCUTERIE ■ **L** OLDEST BUILDING &
DAVOLI **10** CHARCUTERIE-TRAITEUR JEUSSELIN

E

■ CHOCOLATS

FROMAGERIE ■ **R** ■ WINE NICOLAS

RUE VALADON

RUE DUVIVIER

RUE EMEST PSICHARI

CAFE DU MARCHE

LEADER PRICE
BULK SHOPPING

L'EPICERIE FINE **12** **11** ■ ← LOANER BIKES

RUE DU CHAMP DE MARS

← To Eiffel
Tower

REAL ESTATE
AGENCY

13 ARTISAN
BOULANGERIE

14 "A LA MERE DE FAMILLE"
CONFECTIONERY

15
MEPHISTO
SHOE STORE

CLER FLEURS **16**

RUE BOSQUET

R
U
E

BUTCHER ■
BRASSERIE AUX PTT ■

PASSAGE DE LA VIERGE

C
L
E
R

Pedestrian area
(approx. 200 meters in length)

To Army & →
Rodin Museums

↖ N
Not to Scale

CITY INFO
POST

17

AVENUE DE LA MOTTE PICQUET

To Ⓜ Ecole Militaire

TABAC
18 "LA CAVE A CIGARES"

dispatched to merchants with FedEx-like speed and precision. Good luck finding a shopping bag—locals bring their own two-wheeled carts or re-usable bags. Also, notice how the earth-friendly French resist excessive packaging.

Parisians shop with their noses and buy foods in season. Try it. Smell the cheap foreign strawberries (which locals call "plastic straw-berries"), and compare with the odiferous torpedo-shaped French ones *(garriguettes)*. Explore. Find the herbs in the back—is today's delivery in? Check the melons and their country of origin—it must be posted. If they're from Guadeloupe, they're out of season, and many locals won't buy them.

The **Franprix** across the street is a small outpost of a nationwide su-permarket chain. Opposite Grand Hôtel Lévêque is a *traiteur asiatique.* Fast Asian food-to-go—about as common as bakeries—has had an im-pact on traditional Parisian eating habits.

▶ Check out ④ *Le Petit Cler, a trendy café that illustrates how this*

French Etiquette

As you enter a shop, always greet the store owner with *"Bonjour, Ma-dame (or Monsieur)."* Get involved and buy something, but first watch the locals to see if self-service is allowed. Many shopkeepers prefer to serve you and don't want you to touch the goods. If you aren't sure of the protocol, ask, *"Je peux?"* (Can I?; zhuh puh). If you know what you want, point to your choice and say, *"S'il vous plaît"* (Please; see voo play). And don't forget *"Merci beaucoup"* (Thank you very much; mehr-see boh-koo). As you leave, say goodbye with *"Au revoir, Madame (or Monsieur)."*

On your walk, you'll likely see Parisian friends greeting each other with "Le French Kiss" *(faire la bise)*. This cheek-pecking is preferred to the American-style hug. They touch cheeks, pucker their lips, and make a gentle smacking sound—but the lips don't actually touch the cheek. Parisians *faire la bise* with two kisses—first by going left (so the right cheeks almost touch), then right—but some add more kisses. If it happens to you, my recommendation is to go for two with confidence, and then—hover and wait.

once-working-class market street is becoming increasingly upscale. Continue to...

❺ Wine Bacchus

After they've assembled their meal at other stores, shoppers come here to pick the appropriate wine. The clerk is a counselor who works with your menu and budget, and he can put a bottle of white in "Le Chiller" and have it cooled for you in three minutes. The wine is classified by region. Most "Parisians" (born elsewhere) have an affinity for the wines of their home region. You can get a fine bottle (especially the wines of the month in the center) for €12 (open until 20:30 except Sun).

▶ *Next door, smell the...*

❻ *Fromagerie*

Spilling outside into the street, this cheese shop offers more than 200

A cheese for every day of the year

Parisians often shop daily.

types of French cheese, both cow *(vache)* and goat *(chèvre)*. The place is lab-coat-serious but friendly. Known as a "BOF," it's where people buy *beurre, oeuf,* and *fromage*—butter, eggs, and cheese.

Notice the many cheese shapes—wedges, cylinders, balls, and miniature hockey pucks, all powdered white, gray, and burnt marshmallow. It's a festival of mold. The shape tells the buyer where the cheese is from—e.g., a pyramid is from the Loire region. This information is crucial. The region creates the *terroir*—the physical and magical union of sun, soil, and farmer love—that gives the cheese its personality. *Ooh la la* means you're impressed. More *las* means you're more impressed. *Ooh la la la la.* A Parisian friend once held the stinkiest glob close to her nose, took an orgasmic breath, and exhaled, "Yes, it smells like zee feet of angels."

In the back room, they store *les meules,* the big, 170-pound wheels of cheese made from 250 gallons of milk. Although you don't eat the skin of these "hard" cheeses, the skin on most smaller cheeses—the Brie, the Camembert—is part of the taste. "It completes the package," says my local friend.

If you order a set menu at dinner tonight, you can take the cheese course just before or instead of dessert. On a good cheese plate you have a hard cheese (perhaps a Comté, similar to a white cheddar), a softer cheese (maybe Brie or Camembert), a bleu cheese, and a goat cheese—ideally from different regions. Because it's strongest, the goat cheese is usually eaten last.

▸ *Across the street, find the fish shop, known as the...*

➐ *Poissonnerie*

Fresh fish is brought into Paris daily from ports on the English Channel, 110 miles away. In fact, fish here is likely fresher than in many towns closer to the sea—anything wiggling? This *poissonnerie,* like all such shops, was upgraded to meet Europe-wide hygiene standards.

▶ *Next door, check out the doorway (under the awning) at Crêperie Ulysée en Gaule.*

➑ No More Horse Meat

The stones and glass set over the doorway advertise horse meat: *Boucherie Chevaline.* While today this store serves souvlaki and crêpes, the classy 1930s storefront survives from the previous occupant. Signed by the artist, it's a work of art fit for a museum—but it belongs right here.

The door is decorated with lunch coupon decals (like *chèque déjeuner*) for local workers. In France, an employee lunch-subsidy program is an expected perk. Employers get a tax break for issuing voucher checks (worth about €8 each) for each day an employee works in a month. Sack lunches are rare, since a good lunch is sacred.

▶ *A few steps farther, across the street, is the* ➒ **pharmacy.** *In France, mildly sick people go first to the pharmacist, who has authority to diagnose and prescribe certain drugs.*

➓ Oldest Building and Charcuterie-Traiteur Jeusselin

Next to the pharmacy is Rue Cler's oldest building (with the two garret windows on the roof). It's from the early 1800s, when this street was part of a village near Paris and lined with structures like this.

Occupying the ground floor of this house is Charcuterie-Traiteur Jeusselin—a gourmet deli selling mouthwatering food to go. Because Parisian kitchens are so small, many Parisians—even great cooks—rely on these places for beautifully prepared side dishes to complement their home-cooked main course.

Charcuteries by definition are pork butchers, specializing in sausage, pâté, and ham. The charcuterie business is fiercely competitive. Jeusselin proudly displays its hard-won cooking-contest awards on the back wall.

Even with such credentials, to stay competitive many charcuteries have had to add *traiteur* services: prepared dishes, pastries, and wines-to-go. Jeusselin and its rival **Davoli** (across the street) go tête à tête, cooking up *plats du jour* (specials of the day).

Note the system: Order, take your ticket to the cashier to pay, and return with the receipt to pick up your food. To get the freshest food (e.g., a freshly roasted chicken on a spit), come just before lunch and dinner—around 11:00 or 17:00, when Parisians buy provisions for that day's meals.

▶ *A few doors down is...*

⓫ Café du Marché and More

Café du Marché, on the corner, is *the* place to sit and enjoy the action (✪ see page 188). It's Rue Cler's living room, where locals gather before heading home, many staying for a relaxed and affordable dinner. The owner has priced his menu so that residents can afford to dine out on a regular basis, and it works—many patrons eat here five days a week. For a reasonable meal, grab a chair and check the chalk menu listing the *plat du jour.* Notice how the no-smoking-indoors laws have made outdoor seating and propane heaters a huge hit.

The sterile **Leader Price grocery store** (across the street) is a Parisian micro-Costco, selling bulk items. But because storage space is so limited in Parisian apartments, few locals shop here. They buy their nonperishables online, pick up produce three times a week, and buy fresh bread daily. The *moderne* exterior of this store suggests a sneaky bending of Rue Cler's normally rigorous design review for building permits.

▶ *From Café du Marché, hook right and side-trip a couple doors down Rue du Champ de Mars to...*

⓬ L'Epicerie Fine

This fine-foods boutique stands out because of its gentle owners, Pascal and Nathalie. Their mission in life is to explain to travelers, in fluent English, what the French fuss over food is all about. They'll tempt you with fine gourmet treats, Berthillon ice cream, and generous tastes of caramel, balsamic vinegar, and French and Italian olive oils.

▶ *Return to Rue Cler. The neighborhood bakery on the corner is often marked by a line of people waiting to pick up their daily baguette.*

⓭ Artisan Boulangerie

Since the French Revolution, the government has regulated the cost of a basic baguette. And to call your shop a *boulangerie,* by law you must do the baking on the premises. Locals debate the merits of Paris' many *boulangeries.* Some like their baguette a well done while others prefer it more doughy. It's said that a baker cannot be both good at bread and good at pastry—at cooking school, they generally major in one or the other. At Artisan Boulangerie, the baker bucks the trend and seems equally skilled in the two specialties, and Rue Cler regulars agree.

▶ *A bit farther along is...*

⑭ A la Mère de Famille Confectionery

This shop has been in the neighborhood for 30 years. The owner sells modern treats but has always kept the traditional candies, too. "The old ladies, they want the same sweets that made them so happy 80 years ago," she says. You can buy "naked bonbons" right out of the jar and chocolate by the piece (about €0.75 each). You're welcome to assemble a small assortment.

Until a few years ago, the chocolate was dipped and decorated right on the premises. As was the tradition in Rue Cler shops, the merchants resided and produced in the back and sold in the front.

▶ *Next door is a popular French-owned chain store,* ⑮ ***Mephisto Shoes.*** *In a city where many people don't own cars, good shoes matter. The average Parisian walks to the Métro, to work, to shop, and up the stairs to their apartment. Few Parisians join gyms. Across the street you'll find...*

⑯ Cler Fleurs

Almost all Parisians who reside in the city center live in apartments or condos, with no yard. So Parisians spend small fortunes bringing nature into their homes with plants and fresh flower arrangements. Notice the flower boxes on balconies—you work with what you have.

The **butcher shop** a few doors down shows how far Parisians venture from beef when it comes to meat. You'll find rabbit, lamb, duck, veal, pigeon, pig's ears, liver, brain, and tripe—very photogenic.

▶ *Walk on to the end of Rue Cler, where it hits a bigger street flooded with cars and buses.*

⑰ City Info Post

An electronic signpost (10 feet up) directs residents to websites for local information—transportation changes, surveys, employment opportunities, community events, and so on. Notice the big glass recycling bin nearby and the see-through garbage sacks. In the 1990s, there was a rash of nasty incidents where bad guys put rigged camp-stove canisters into metal garbage cans, which exploded into deadly shrapnel. Authorities solved the problem by replacing the metal cans with translucent bags.

▸ *Across the busy Avenue de la Motte-Picquet is a* tabac.

⑱ Tabac La Cave à Cigares

Just as the US has liquor stores licensed to sell booze, the only place for people over 16 to buy tobacco legally in France is at a *tabac* (tah-bah) counter. Notice how European laws require a bold warning sign on cigarettes—about half the size of the package—that says, bluntly, *fumer tue* (smoking kills).

A *tabac* sells more than just tobacco, and is a much-appreciated fixture of Parisian neighborhoods. It's a kind of government cash desk, selling stamps, public-transit tickets, and the always-popular LOTO tickets. Locals pay for parking meters by buying a card...or pay their fines here if they don't.

American smokers may not be able to resist the temptation to pick up a *petit* Corona—your chance to buy a fine Cuban cigar.

▸ *The Ecole Militaire Métro stop is just down Avenue de la Motte-Picquet to the right. If you bought a picnic along this walk, here are two good places to enjoy it: Leaving Rue Cler, turn left on Avenue de la Motte-Picquet for the Army Museum (find the small park after crossing Boulevard de la Tour-Maubourg). Or, turn right to reach the Champ de Mars park (and the Eiffel Tower).*

Versailles Tour

Château de Versailles

Every king's dream, Versailles (vehr-"sigh") was the residence of French monarchs and the cultural heartbeat of Europe for about 100 years. The powerful court of Louis XIV at Versailles set the standard of culture for all of Europe, right up to modern times.

Versailles has three blockbuster sights. The palace itself—the Château—features the lavish, chandeliered rooms of France's kings. The expansive Gardens are a landscaped wonderland of statues and fountains. Finally, the Trianon Palaces and Domaine de Marie-Antoinette offer a pastoral getaway of small palaces, including Marie's faux-peasant Hamlet.

ORIENTATION

Cost: Buy either a Paris Museum Pass or a Versailles Le Passeport Pass, both of which give you access to the most important parts of the complex. If you don't get a pass, buy individual tickets for each of the three sections:

- **The Château:** €18 (free on first Sun Nov-March).
- **The Trianon Palaces and Domaine de Marie-Antoinette:** €12 (free on first Sun Nov-March).
- **The Gardens:** Free, except on Spectacle days, when admission is €9.

Passes: The **Paris Museum Pass** covers the Château and the Trianon/Domaine area (a €30 value), but doesn't include the Gardens on Spectacle days.

The **Le Passeport Pass** (€20 for one day, €25 for two days) covers the Château and the Trianon/Domaine area. On Spectacle days, its €27 for one day, €30 for two.

Buying Passes and Tickets: Ideally, buy your ticket or pass before arriving at Versailles. You can purchase tickets at any Paris TI, FNAC department store, or at www.chateauversailles.fr (print out your pass/ticket). If you arrive in Versailles without a pass or a ticket, you can buy it at the rarely crowded Versailles TI, not far from the train station (10 percent fee).

Your last and (usually) worst option is to buy a pass or ticket at the busy Château ticket-sales office (to the left as you face the palace). Ticket windows accept American credit cards. If there's a line, you can use the ticket machines at the back of the room (requires chip-and-PIN card or bills).

Hours: The **Château** is open April-Oct Tue-Sun 8:30-19:00, Nov-March Tue-Sun 9:00-17:30, closed Mon year-round.

The **Trianon Palaces and Domaine de Marie-Antoinette** are open April-Oct Tue-Sun 12:00-18:30, Nov-March until 17:30, last entry 45 minutes before closing, closed Mon year-round (off-season only the two Trianon Palaces and the Hamlet are open, not other outlying buildings).

The **Gardens** are open April-Oct daily 8:00-20:30; Nov-March until 18:00.

Crowd-Beating Strategies: Versailles is a zoo May-Sept 9:30-13:00, so come early or late. Avoid Sundays, Tuesdays, and Saturdays (in that order), when the place is jammed with a slow shuffle of tourists from open to close. To skip the ticket-buying line, buy tickets or passes in advance, or book a guided tour. Unfortunately, all ticket holders—including those with advance tickets and passes—must go through the often-slow security checkpoint at the Château's courtyard entry and again at the Château entrance (longest lines 10:00-12:00). Consider seeing the Gardens during midmorning and the Château in the afternoon, when crowds die down.

Here's how I'd spend the day at Versailles: Leave Paris by 7:45 to beat the crowds. Tour the Château, then break for lunch in the Gardens. Spend the afternoon touring the Gardens and the Trianon/Domaine. Have dinner in Versailles town, then head back to Paris.

Pickpockets: Assume pickpockets are working the tourist crowds.

Getting There: The town of Versailles is 35 minutes southwest of Paris. Take the **RER-C train** (4/hour, €7.10 round-trip) from any of these Paris RER stops: Gare d'Austerlitz, St. Michel, Musée d'Orsay, Invalides, Pont de l'Alma, or Champ de Mars. At the RER station, catch any train listed as "Versailles Château Rive Gauche" (abbreviated to "Versailles Chât" or "Versailles RG"). Get off at the last stop (Versailles Château R.G., or "Rive Gauche"). Exit through the turnstiles (you may need to insert your ticket). To reach the Château, turn right out of the station, then left at the first boulevard, and walk 10 minutes. To return to Paris, catch any train—they serve all downtown Paris RER stops on the C line. **Taxis** for the 30-minute ride (without traffic) cost about €60.

Information: Tel. 01 30 83 78 00. Check the excellent website for updates and special events—www.chateauversailles.fr. The uncrowded city **Tourist Office** is in town on your walk from the RER station to the palace—it's just past the Pullman Hôtel (daily 9:00-19:00, Sun until 18:00, shorter hours in winter, tel. 01 39 24 88 88). The Château's information office is on the left side of the courtyard as you face the Château (WCs, toll tel. 08 10 81 16 14).

Tours: The 1.5-hour English **guided tour** gives you access to a few extra rooms and lets you skip the regular security line (€7, plus €15 palace entry if you don't have it). Book online or immediately upon arrival at the guided-tours office (to the right of the Château—look for yellow *Visites Conferences* signs). A free **audioguide** to the Château is

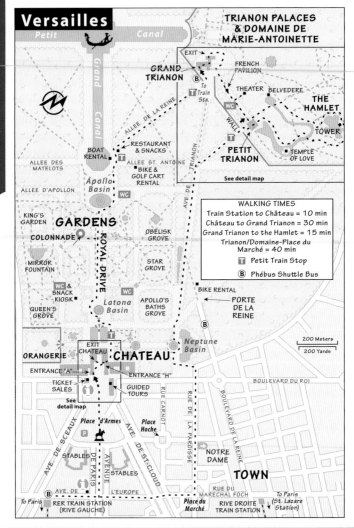

Versailles

TRIANON PALACES
& DOMAINE DE
MARIE-ANTOINETTE

Petit   Canal

Grand Canal

EXIT

GRAND TRIANON

B To Train Stn.

FRENCH PAVILION

THEATER   BELVEDERE

THE HAMLET

WC

TOWER

ALLEE DE LA REINE

WALL

PETIT TRIANON

TEMPLE OF LOVE

ALLEE DES MATELOTS

BOAT RENTAL

RESTAURANT & SNACKS

ALLEE ST. ANTOINE

BIKE & GOLF CART RENTAL

AVE. DE TRIANON

See detail map

ALLEE D'APOLLON

Apollo Basin

WC

KING'S GARDEN

GARDENS

COLONNADE

OBELISK GROVE

ROYAL DRIVE

MIRROR FOUNTAIN

STAR GROVE

WALKING TIMES
Train Station to Château = 10 min
Château to Grand Trianon = 30 min
Grand Trianon to the Hamlet = 15 min
Trianon/Domaine-Place du Marché = 40 min
T Petit Train Stop
B Phébus Shuttle Bus

WC & SNACK KIOSK

QUEEN'S GROVE

Latona Basin

WC

APOLLO'S BATHS GROVE

BIKE RENTAL

PORTE DE LA REINE

B

Neptune Basin

200 Meters
200 Yards

ORANGERIE

EXIT CHATEAU

CHATEAU

ENTRANCE "A"

ENTRANCE "H"

BOULEVARD DU ROI

TICKET SALES

GUIDED TOURS

See detail map

RUE CARNOT

RUE DE LA PAROISSE

BOULEVARD DE LA REINE

Place d'Armes

Place Hoche

P

NOTRE DAME

AVE. DE SCEAUX

AVE. DE PARIS

AVENUE DE ST-CLOUD

STABLES

STABLES

TOWN

AVE. DE L'EUROPE

RUE DU MARECHAL FOCH

B

To Paris

RER TRAIN STATION (RIVE GAUCHE)

Place du Marché

RIVE DROITE TRAIN STATION

To Paris (St. Lazare Station)

Rick Steves | Pocket Paris

included in admission. Other podcasts and digital tours are available in the "multimedia" section at www.chateauversailles.fr. Or you can ∩ download a free Rick Steves **audio tour** (✪ see page 207).

Length of This Day Trip: With the usual lines, allow 1.5 hours each for the Château, the Gardens (includes time for lunch), and the Trianon/Domaine. Add another two hours for round-trip transit, and you're looking at nearly an eight-hour day.

Baggage Check: To enter the Château and the two Trianons, you must use the free baggage check for large bags and baby strollers (just after the Château entrance security check).

Services: WCs are plentiful and well-signed in the Château. Those in the Gardens are farther and fewer between.

Eating: The $ Grand Café d'Orléans, to the left of the Château, offers good-value self-service meals (sandwiches and small salads, great for picnicking in the Gardens). In the Gardens, you'll find several cafés and snack stands. One is located near the Latona Fountain (less crowded) and others are in an atmospheric cluster at the Grand Canal (more crowds and more choices, including two restaurants).

In Versailles town center, several colorful eateries line lively Place du Marché Notre-Dame, or along traffic-free Rue de Satory. Handy McDonald's and Starbucks (both with WCs) are near the train station.

Photography: Allowed, but no flash indoors.

Spectacles in the Gardens: On certain days in spring and summer, piped-in classical music accompanies impressive fountain displays. The fountains run late March-Oct Sat-Sun 11:00-12:00 & 15:30-17:00, plus Tue mid-May-June and Fri late March-early May, same hours. On these spray days, the Gardens cost €9. On other Tue in-season you get all-day music, but no water (€8). Elaborate sound-and-light displays are staged on Sat nights (and some Fri) mid-June-mid-Sept at 20:30 (€20-41). The schedule changes; see the full calendar at www.chateauversailles.fr.

Starring: Luxurious palaces, endless gardens, Louis XIV, Marie-Antoinette, and the *ancien régime.*

THE TOUR BEGINS

▶ *Stand in the huge courtyard and face the palace. The ticket-sales office is to the left. The entrance to the Château (once you have your ticket or pass) is marked Entrance A.*

On this self-guided tour, we'll see the Château, the landscaped Gardens in the "backyard," and the Trianon Palaces and Domaine de Marie-Antoinette, located at the far end of the Gardens.

The Original Château and the Courtyard

The section of the palace with the clock is the original Château, once a small hunting lodge where little Louis XIV spent his happiest boyhood years. Naturally, the Sun King's private bedroom (the three arched windows beneath the clock) faced the rising sun. The palace and grounds are laid out on an east–west axis.

Once king, Louis XIV expanded the lodge by attaching wings, creating the present U-shape. Later, the long north and south wings were built. The total cost of the project has been estimated at half of France's entire GNP for one year.

Think how busy this courtyard must have been 300 years ago. As many as 5,000 nobles were here at any one time, each with an entourage. They'd buzz from games to parties to amorous rendezvous in sedan-chair taxis. Servants ran about delivering secret messages and roast legs of lamb. Horse-drawn carriages arrived at the fancy gate with their finely dressed passengers, having driven up the broad boulevard that ran directly from Paris. Then, as now, there were hordes of tourists, pickpockets, palace workers, and men selling wind-up children's toys.

Entrance A—security checkpoint

Original Château and courtyard

We Three Kings

Versailles was the residence of the king and the seat of France's government for a hundred years. With 18 million people united under one king (England had only 5.5 million), a booming economy, and a powerful military, France was Europe's number-one power. Versailles was the cultural heartbeat of Europe. Everyone learned French. French taste in clothes, hairstyles, table manners, theater, music, art, and kissing spread across the Continent.

Three kings lived in Versailles during its century of glory:

Louis XIV (reigned 1643-1715), Europe's greatest king, built Versailles and established French dominance.

Louis XV (r. 1715-1774) was his great-grandson. (Louis XIV reigned for 72 years, outliving several heirs.) Louis XV carried on the tradition and policies, but without the Sun King's flair. France's power abroad was weakening, and there were rumblings of rebellion from within.

Louis XVI (r. 1774-1792)—a shy, meek bookworm—inherited a nation in crisis. He married a sweet girl from the Austrian royal family, Marie-Antoinette, and together they retreated into the idyllic gardens of Versailles while revolutionary fires smoldered.

▶ *After passing through security at Entrance A, you spill out into the open-air courtyard inside the golden Royal Gate. Enter the Château, where you'll find an info desk (get a map), WCs, and bag check. Glance through a doorway at the impressive Royal Chapel, which we'll see again upstairs.*

Just follow the flow of crowds through a number of rooms (the route and exhibits change frequently). Climb the stairs and pass through more exhibits. Finally, you reach a palatial golden-brown room, with a doorway that overlooks the Royal Chapel.

Royal Chapel

Dut-dutta-dah! Every morning at 10:00, the musicians struck up the music, these big golden doors opened, and Louis XIV and his family stepped onto the balcony to attend Mass. While Louis looked down on the golden altar, the lowly nobles on the ground floor knelt with their backs to the altar and looked up—worshipping Louis worshipping God. Important religious ceremonies took place here, including the marriage of young Louis XVI to Marie-Antoinette.

In the vast pagan "temple" that is Versailles—built to glorify one man, Louis XIV—this Royal Chapel is a paltry tip of the hat to that "other" god... the Christian one.

▶ *Enter the next room, an even more sumptuous space with a fireplace and a colorful painting on the ceiling.*

Hercules Drawing Room

Pleasure ruled. The main suppers, balls, and receptions were held in this room. Picture elegant partygoers in fine silks, wigs, rouge, lipstick, and

The Royal Chapel, where Louis XIV worshipped and allowed himself to be worshipped

Versailles Château

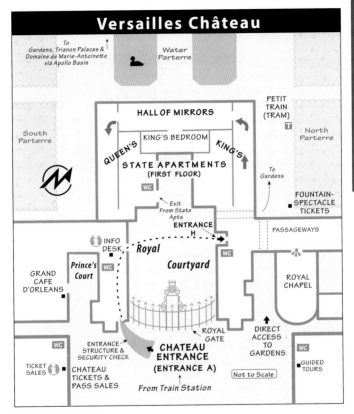

To Gardens, Trianon Palaces & Domaine de Marie-Antoinette via Apollo Basin

Water Parterre

PETIT TRAIN (TRAM)

North Parterre

HALL OF MIRRORS

KING'S BEDROOM

QUEEN'S

KING'S

South Parterre

STATE APARTMENTS (FIRST FLOOR)

WC

To Gardens

FOUNTAIN-SPECTACLE TICKETS

Exit From State Apts

ENTRANCE H

PASSAGEWAYS

WC

INFO DESK

Royal

WC

Prince's Court

Courtyard

GRAND CAFE D'ORLEANS

ROYAL CHAPEL

DIRECT ACCESS TO GARDENS

ROYAL GATE

CHATEAU ENTRANCE (ENTRANCE A)

ENTRANCE STRUCTURE & SECURITY CHECK

WC

TICKET SALES

CHATEAU TICKETS & PASS SALES

From Train Station

Not to Scale

WC

GUIDED TOURS

fake moles (and that's just the men), as they dance to the strains of a string quartet.

On the wall opposite the fireplace is an appropriate painting showing Christ in the middle of a Venetian party. The work by Paolo Veronese was one of Louis XIV's favorites, so they decorated the room around it. Stand by the fireplace for the full effect: The room's columns, arches, and frieze match the height and style of Veronese's painted architecture, which makes the painting an extension of the room.

Louis XIV—The Sun King

Louis XIV was a true Renaissance Man, a century after the Renaissance: athletic, good-looking, a musician, dancer, horseman, statesman, art lover, lover. He was a good listener who could put even commoners at ease.

Louis XIV, age 63, by Hyacinthe Rigaud

Louis had grown up in the previous royal residence—the Louvre in Paris. When he became king, he moved the government to the forests of Versailles, where he'd hunted as a kid. There, he could concentrate power around himself. He invited France's nobles—who in other countries were the center of power—to live at Versailles. They became virtual slaves of pleasure, dependent on Louis' generosity, while he made the important decisions.

Louis called himself the Sun King because he gave life and warmth to all he touched. He was also thought of as Apollo, the Greek god of the sun. Versailles became the personal temple of this god on earth, decorated with statues and symbols of Apollo, the sun, and Louis XIV himself.

For 70 years, he was the perfect embodiment of the absolute monarch. He summed it up best himself with his famous rhyme—"*L'état, c'est moi!*" (lay-tah say-mwah): "The state, that's me!"

The ceiling painting creates the effect of a sunroof opening up to heaven. Hercules (with his club) hurries up to heaven on a chariot, late for his wedding to the king of the gods' daughter. The scene echoes real life—Louis XIV built the room for his own daughter's wedding reception.

▶ *From here on it's a one-way tour—getting lost is not allowed. Follow the crowds into the small green room with a goddess in pink on the ceiling. The names of the rooms generally come from the paintings on the ceilings.*

Salon of Abundance

If the party in the Hercules Room got too intense, you could always step in here for some refreshments. Silver trays were loaded up with liqueurs, exotic stimulants (coffee), juice, chocolates, and, on really special occasions, three-bean salad.

Louis XIV was a gracious host who enjoyed letting his hair down at night. If he took a liking to you, he might sneak you through those doors there (in the middle of the wall) and into his own private study, where he'd show off his collection of dishes, medals, jewels, or...the *Mona Lisa,* which hung on his wall.

Venus Room

Love ruled at Versailles. In this room, couples would cavort beneath the goddess of love, floating on the ceiling. Venus sends down a canopy of golden garlands to ensnare mortals in delicious *amour.* Notice how in the paintings at both ends of the room, the painted columns match the room's real ones, extending this grand room into mythical courtyards. Baroque artists loved to mix their media to fool the eye.

Don't let the statue of a confident Louis XIV as a Roman emperor fool you. He started out as a poor little rich kid with a chip on his shoulder. The French *parlements* treated little Louis and his mother as virtual prisoners in their home, the Royal Palace in Paris (today's Louvre). There they eked by with bland meals, hand-me-down leotards, and pointed shoes. After Louis XIV attained power and wealth, he made Versailles a pleasure palace—his way of saying that "Living well is the best revenge."

Hercules among the gods

Venus Room ceiling painting

Diana Room

Here in the billiards room, Louis and his men played on a table that stood in the center of the room, while ladies sat surrounding them on Persian-carpet cushions, and music wafted in from next door. Louis was a good pool player, a sore loser, and a king—thus, he rarely lost.

The famous bust of Louis by Giovanni Lorenzo Bernini (in the center) shows a handsome, dashing, 27-year-old playboy-king. His gaze is steady amid his windblown cloak and hair. Young Louis loved life. He hunted animals by day (notice Diana the Huntress, with her bow, on the ceiling) and chased beautiful women at night.

Games were actually an important part of Louis' political strategy, known as "the domestication of the nobility." By distracting the nobles with the pleasures of courtly life, he was free to run the government his way. Gambling was popular (especially a blackjack-type card game), and Louis lent money to the losers, making them even more indebted to him. The good life was an addiction, and Louis kept the medicine cabinet well-stocked.

As you move into the next room, notice the fat walls that hid thin servants, who were to be at their master's constant call—but out of sight when not needed.

Mars Room

This red room, home to Louis' Swiss bodyguards, has a military flair. On the ceiling there's Mars, the Greek god of war, in a chariot pulled by wolves. As you wander, remember that most of the carpets, mirrors, furniture, and tapestries we see today are not original, but are from the same period.

Venus Room—Louis XIV as emperor

Mercury Room—the king's official bedroom

Mercury Room

Louis' life was a work of art. Everything he did was a public event designed to show his subjects how it should be done. This room may have served as Louis' official (not actual) bedroom, where the Sun King would ritually rise each morning to warm his subjects.

From a canopied bed (like this 18th-century one), Louis would get up, dress, and take a seat for morning prayer. Meanwhile, the nobles would stand behind a balustrade, in awe of his piety, nobility, and clean socks. At breakfast they murmured with delight as he deftly decapitated his boiled egg with a knife. And when Louis went to bed at night, the dukes and barons would fight over who got to hold the candle while he slipped into his royal jammies.

Apollo Room

This was the grand throne room. Louis held court from a 10-foot-tall, silver-and-gold, canopied throne on a raised platform placed in the center of the room.

Everything in here reminds us of Louis XIV's glory. On the ceiling the sun god Apollo (representing Louis) drives his chariot, dragging the sun across the heavens to warm the four corners of the world—including good ol' America, symbolized by an Indian maiden with a crocodile.

The famous portrait by Hyacinthe Rigaud over the fireplace gives a more human look at Louis XIV, age 63. He's shown in a dancer's pose, displaying the legs that made him one of the all-time dancing fools of kingery. At night they often held parties in this room, actually dancing around the throne. Louis had more than 300 wigs like this one. The fashion sprouted all over Europe, even spreading to the American colonies.

Louis XIV may have been treated like a god, but his subjects adored him as a symbol of everything a man could be, the fullest expression of the Renaissance Man.

▶ *Continue into the final room of the King's Wing.*

War Room

"Louis Quatorze was addicted to wars," and the room depicts his victories—in marble, gilding, stucco, and paint. On the ceiling, Lady France hurls down thunderbolts at her enemies. The stucco relief on the wall shows Louis XIV on horseback, triumphing over his fallen enemies. But

Louis' greatest triumph may be the next room, the one that everybody wrote home about.

Hall of Mirrors

No one had ever seen anything like this hall when it was opened. Mirrors were still a great luxury at the time, and the number and size of these monsters was astounding. The hall is nearly 250 feet long. There are 17 arched mirrors, matched by 17 windows letting in that breathtaking view of the Gardens. Lining the hall are 24 gilded candelabra, eight busts of Roman emperors, and eight classical-style statues (seven of them ancient). The ceiling shows Louis in the central panel doing what he did best—triumphing.

Imagine this place lit by the flames of thousands of candles, filled with ambassadors, nobles, and guests dressed in silks and powdered wigs. At the far end of the room sits the king, on the canopied throne moved in temporarily from the Apollo Room. Servants glide by with silver trays of hors d'oeuvres, and an orchestra fuels the festivities. The mirrors reflect an

The Hall of Mirrors—a grand ballroom of chandeliers, mirrored walls, and staggering views

age when beautiful people loved to look at themselves. It was no longer a sin to be proud of good looks or to enjoy the good things in life: laughing, dancing, eating, drinking, flirting, and watching the sun set into the distant canal.

From the center of the hall you can fully appreciate the epic scale of Versailles. The huge palace (by architect Louis Le Vau), the fantasy interior (by Charles Le Brun), and the endless Gardens (by André Le Nôtre) made Versailles *le* best. In 1919, Germany and the Allies signed the Treaty of Versailles, ending World War I (and, some say, starting World War II) right here, in the Hall of Mirrors.

▶ *Midway down the Hall of Mirrors, you'll be routed to the left through the heart of the palace, to the...*

King's Bedroom and Council Rooms

Pass through a first large room to find Louis XIV's bedroom. It's elaborately decorated with an impressive bed and balustrade, and the decor changed with the season. Look out the window and notice how this small room is at the exact center of the immense horseshoe-shaped building, overlooking the main courtyard and—naturally—facing the rising sun in the east. It symbolized the exact center of power in France. Imagine the humiliation on that day in 1789 when Louis' great-great-great-grandson, Louis XVI, was forced to stand here and acknowledge the angry crowds that filled the square demanding the end of the divine monarchy.

▶ *The Queen's Wing of the Château is closed for extensive renovation, so this ends our tour of the Château. But there is more—the History of France rooms (on this floor) and the modestly furnished Dauphin's and Mesdames Apartments (downstairs).*

King's bedroom—heart of the palace

View down the Royal Drive—eight-mile axis

Exit the palace and follow signs to the Gardens (les Jardins), located behind the Château.

Consider a lunch break before tackling the Gardens.

THE GARDENS

Louis XIV was a divine-right ruler. One way he proved it was by controlling nature like a god. These lavish grounds—elaborately planned, pruned, and decorated—showed everyone that Louis was in total command.

The Gardens are vast. For some, a stroll through the landscaped shrubs around the Château and quick view down the Royal Drive is plenty. But it's worth the 10-minute walk down the Royal Drive to the Apollo Basin and back (even if you don't continue on to the Trianon/Domaine).

▶ *Entering the Gardens, make your way farther into the king's spacious backyard until you reach the top step of a staircase overlooking the Gardens. Face away from the palace and take in the jaw-dropping...*

The Latona Basin fountain—symbolic of Louis the XIV's early childhood

Getting Around the Gardens

On Foot: It's a 45-minute walk (plus sightseeing) from the palace, down to the Grand Canal, past the two Trianon palaces, to the Hamlet at the far end of Domaine de Marie-Antoinette.

By Bike: There's a bike rental station by the Grand Canal (€8/hour, daily 10:00-18:30). You can't take your bike inside the grounds of the Trianon/Domaine, but you can park it near an entrance.

By *Petit Train*: The very slow-moving tram makes a one-way loop from the Château (north side) to the Grand and Petit Trianons, Grand Canal, and back to the Château (€7.50 round-trip, Tue-Sun 10:00-18:00, Mon 11:00-17:00, shorter hours in winter).

By Golf Cart: These are fun, but you can't take them inside the Trianon/Domaine and they only go along a prescribed route (€32/hour, steep late fees, rent just behind the Château, near the *petit train* stop, or at Grand Canal).

View Down the Royal Drive

This, to me, is the most stunning spot in all of Versailles. With the palace behind you, it seems as if the grounds stretch out forever. Versailles was laid out along an eight-mile axis that included the grounds, the palace, and the town of Versailles itself, one of the first instances of urban planning since Roman times and a model for future capitals, such as Washington, D.C. and Brasília.

Looking down the Royal Drive, you see the round Apollo fountain in the distance. Just beyond that is the Grand Canal. The groves on either side of the Royal Drive were planted with trees from all over, laid out in an elaborate grid, and dotted with statues and fountains. Of the original 1,500 fountains, 300 remain.

▶ *Stroll down the steps to get a good look at the frogs and lizards that fill the round...*

Latona Basin

Atop the fountain stands Apollo (the sun god) and his sister (Diana) as little kids, with their mom, Latona. Latona, an unwed mother, was insulted by the local peasants, so Zeus swooped down and turned them into frogs and lizards.

▶ *As you walk down past the basin toward the Royal Drive, you'll pass by "ancient" statues done by 17th-century French sculptors. Our next stop—the Colonnade—is hidden in the woods on the left side of the Royal Drive, about three-fourths of the way to the Apollo Basin.*

Colonnade

Versailles had no prestigious ancient ruins, so the king built this prefab Roman ruin—a 100-foot circle of 64 red-marble columns supporting pure-white arches. Nobles would picnic in the shade, watching the birdbath fountains spout, listening to a string quartet and pretending they were enlightened citizens of the ancient world.

Apollo Basin

The fountains of Versailles were its most famous attraction, and this one of the sun god—Louis XIV—was the centerpiece. Louis, in his sunny chariot,

The Apollo Basin: The sun god rises from the mist on days when the fountains play.

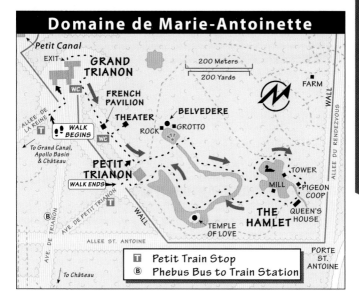

Domaine de Marie-Antoinette

Petit Canal
EXIT
GRAND TRIANON
Petit Canal
WC
200 Meters
200 Yards
FARM
WALL
ALLEE DE LA REINE
FRENCH PAVILION
THEATER
WALK BEGINS
WC
BELVEDERE
ROCK
GROTTO
To Grand Canal,
Apollo Basin
& Château
PETIT TRIANON
WALK ENDS
ALLEE DU RENDEZVOUS
TOWER
MILL
PIGEON COOP
ALLEE DE PETIT TRIANON
AVE. DE PETIT TRIANON
WALL
THE HAMLET
QUEEN'S HOUSE
B
AVE. DE TRIANON
ALLEE ST. ANTOINE
TEMPLE OF LOVE
PORTE ST. ANTOINE
To Château

🚃 **Petit Train Stop**
Ⓑ **Phebus Bus to Train Station**

starts his journey across the sky. The horses are half-submerged, giving the impression, when the fountains play, of the sun rising out of the mists of dawn.

All the fountains are gravity-powered. They work on the same principle as blocking a hose with your finger to make it squirt. Underground streams (pumped into Versailles by Seine River pressure) feed into smaller pipes at the fountains, which shoot the water high into the air.

Looking back at the palace from here, realize that the distance you just walked is only a fraction of this vast complex of buildings, gardens, and waterways. Be glad you don't have to mow the lawn.

Grand Canal

In an era before virtual reality, this was the next best thing to an actual trip to Venice. Couples in gondolas would pole along the waters accompanied by barges with orchestras playing "O Sole Mio." The canal is one mile from end to end.

These days, the Grand Canal hosts eateries, rental boats, bike and golf-cart rentals, and a *petit train* tram stop.

▶ *The area called the Trianon Palaces and Domaine de Marie-Antoinette is a 10-minute walk from the Grand Canal. There are three entrances to the walled enclosure: near the Grand Trianon palace (where we'll enter), near the Petit Trianon palace, or near the Hamlet.*

To get to the Grand Trianon, veer right just past the restaurants and boat rental (✪ see the map on page 139) and follow the dirt path along a looooong strip of lawn. This leads uphill 500 yards to the Grand Trianon.

TRIANON PALACES AND DOMAINE DE MARIE-ANTOINETTE

Versailles began as an escape from the pressures of kingship. But in a short time, the Château became as stressful as Paris ever was—with sniping politics, strict etiquette, and 24/7 scrutiny. Louis XIV and his successors needed an escape from their escape, so they built this fantasy world of palaces and pleasure gardens and retreated further and further from everyday life.

Grand Trianon

Delicate, pink, and set amid gardens, the Grand Trianon was the perfect summer getaway. This was the king's private residence away from the main palace. He spent a couple of nights a week here, near the tiny peasant village of Trianon—hence the name.

Louis XIV's bedroom: Wake up with the king.

Grand Trianon—gardens in back

French Pavilion—one of many hidden gems

Inside, the rooms are a complex overlay of furnishings from many different kings, dauphins, and nobles who lived here over the centuries. Louis XIV alone had three different bedrooms. Concentrate on the illustrious time of Louis XIV (1688-1715) and Napoleon Bonaparte (1810-1814).

The spacious **Mirror Room** (Salon des Glaces) has the original white walls and mirrors of Louis XIV, and the Empire-style furniture of Napoleon (unornamented, high-polished wood, with classical motifs). In **Louis XIV's Bedroom** (Chambre de l'Impératrice), imagine waking up in this big bed with your lover, throwing back the curtain, and looking out the windows at the gardens. Exit into the open-air **colonnade (Peristyle)** that connects the two wings. Originally, this pink-columned passageway had windows, an enormously expensive luxury that allowed visitors to enjoy the gardens even in bad weather.

The **Emperor's Family Drawing Room** (Salon de Famille de l'Empereur) was a theater for Louix XIV, a game room for Louis XV, and

Napoleon's family room. After Napoleon was defeated and France's royalty returned, King Louis-Philippe I lived here. Walk through a series of rooms until you reach the **Malachite Room** (Salon des Malachites). This was Napoleon's living room. You'll see the impressive green basin, vases, and candelabras made of Russian malachite given to Napoleon by Czar Alexander I.

The white, 170-foot-long **Cotelle Gallery** (Galerie Cotelle) was Louis' reception hall. The gallery is interspersed with big French doors and lined with paintings of Versailles vistas, people by promenading aristocrats. Party guests could admire the gardens in the paintings, then step out into the real thing.

▶ ✪ *Use the map on page 139 to explore the rest of the Trianon/Domaine grounds. You'll meander along pathways through woods and gardens that lead you naturally from sight to sight. Exiting the Grand Trianon,*

Belvedere—tiny palace above a pond

The Hamlet—a faux peasant village where Marie-Antoinette indulged her fantasies

Temple of Love—perfect for a rendezvous

circle the building clockwise, then follow signs to the Petit Trianon. *Your first stop is the...*

French Pavilion

This small, white building with rooms fanning out from the center has big French doors to let in a cool breeze. Here Marie-Antoinette spent summer evenings with family and friends, listening to music or playing parlor games, exploring all avenues of *la douceur de vivre*—the sweetness of living.

▸ *Up ahead is the cube-shaped Petit Trianon palace. But midway there, detour left to find...*

▸ Marie-Antoinette's Theater

Marie-Antoinette was an aspiring performer. In this plush, fully functioning, 100-seat dollhouse theater, she and her friends acted out plays for a select audience.

▸ *Just before reaching the Petit Trianon, turn left and find the nearby...*

Belvedere, Rock, and Grotto

The octagonal Belvedere palace is as much windows as it is walls. When the doors were open, it could serve as a gazebo for musicians, serenading nobles in this man-made alpine setting. To the left of the Belvedere is the "Rock," a fake mountain that pours water into the pond. To the right of the Belvedere (you'll have to find it) is the secret Grotto.

▸ *Facing the Belvedere, turn right (east) and follow the pond's meandering stream. Continue frolicking along the paths till you spy a round, fanciful tower and a smattering of rustic, half-timbered buildings fronting a lake—the Hansel-and-Gretel-like...*

Hamlet

Marie-Antoinette longed for the simple life of a peasant—not the hard labor of real peasants, who sweated and starved around her, but the fairy-tale world of simple country pleasures.

This was an actual working farm with a dairy (by the tower), a water mill, a pigeon coop *(Le Colombier)*, and a menagerie where her servants kept cows, goats, chickens, and ducks. The Queen's House—two buildings connected by a wooden skywalk—was like any typical peasant farmhouse, with a billiard room, library, dining hall, and two living rooms.

▶ *As you head back toward the Petit Trianon, you'll pass by the white dome of the...*

Temple of Love

A circle of 12 white marble Corinthian columns supports a dome, decorating a path where lovers could stroll. It's a delightful monument to a society where the rich could afford that ultimate luxury, romantic love.

Petit Trianon

Louis XV built the Petit Trianon ("Small Trianon") at the urging of his first mistress, Madame de Pompadour, and it later became home to his next mistress, Madame du Barry.

The gray, cubical building is a masterpiece of Neoclassical architecture. It has four distinct facades, each a perfect and harmonious combination of Greek-style columns, windows, and railings. You can tour the handsome interior. The Baroque WC was a head of its time.

When Louis XVI became king, he gave the building to his bride Marie-Antoinette. She made it her home and installed a carousel on the lawn outside. Here she played, while in the cafés of faraway Paris, revolutionaries plotted the end of the *ancien régime.*

Petit Trianon—four-faced palace

▶ *The real world and the main Château are a 30-minute walk to the south-east. If you've had enough walking, you can ride the petit train from here back to the Château. Or, to return directly to the Versailles Château Rive Gauche station, catch the TRI line shuttle bus (runs hourly mid-April-Oct only, €2 or one Métro ticket).*

Sights

Paris is blessed with world-class museums and monuments—more than anyone could see in a single visit. To help you prioritize your limited time and money, I've chosen what I think are the best of Paris' many sights. I've clustered them into walkable neighborhoods for more efficient sightseeing.

Definitely consider buying a Paris Museum Pass to save money and skip long ticket-buying lines, and review my other sightseeing tips (✪ see pages 207-208).

Note that some of Paris' biggest sights (marked with a ✪) are described in much more detail in the individual self-guided tour chapters. There you'll also find crucial info on how to avoid lines, save money, and get a decent bite to eat nearby.

HISTORIC CORE OF PARIS

The Historic Core consists of the island in the center of Paris named Île de la Cité, and spills onto the neighboring river banks. Here you'll find sights from Paris' 2,000-year history, with an emphasis on its medieval glory days (Mo: Cité, Hôtel de Ville, or St. Michel).

▲▲▲Notre-Dame Cathedral (Cathédrale Notre-Dame de Paris)

The 850-year-old cathedral of "Our Lady" features winged gargoyles, flying buttresses, a climbable tower, and a solemn interior.

✪ See page 17 in the Historic Paris Walk chapter.

▲▲▲Sainte-Chapelle

Europe's best stained glass—and that's saying something!—makes this small Gothic church glow.

✪ See page 33 in the Historic Paris Walk chapter.

▲Conciergerie

Marie-Antoinette and thousands of others were imprisoned here on their way to the guillotine.

✪ See page 38 in the Historic Paris Walk chapter.

▲Deportation Memorial (Mémorial de la Déportation)

A sober remembrance of the 200,000 French victims of the Nazi concentration camps.

✪ See page 28 in the Historic Paris Walk chapter.

Paris Archaeological Crypt

Visit Roman ruins, trace the street plan of the medieval village, and see diagrams of how early Paris grew. The ruins are a confusing mix of foundations from every time period—the city's oldest rampart, a medieval road, or a Roman building with a heated floor—but interesting multimedia displays help sort them out. Worthwhile if you have a Museum Pass.

▶ *€7, covered by Museum Pass. Open Tue-Sun 10:00-18:00, closed Mon. Enter 100 yards in front of Notre-Dame. Tel. 01 55 42 50 10, www. crypte.paris.fr.*

MAJOR MUSEUMS NEIGHBORHOOD

Paris' grandest park, the Tuileries Garden, today links the Louvre, Orangerie, and Orsay museums. All of these are less than a 20-minute walk apart (Mo: Palais Royal–Musée du Louvre and Concorde; RER-C: Musée d'Orsay).

▲▲▲Louvre (Musée du Louvre)
Europe's oldest, biggest, greatest, and second-most-crowded museum (after the Vatican) is home to *Mona Lisa, Venus de Milo,* and the rest of Western Civilization.
✪ See the Louvre Tour on page 43.

▲▲▲Orsay Museum (Musée d'Orsay)
Europe's greatest collection of Impressionism (Manet, Monet, Renoir), Post-Impressionism (Van Gogh, Cézanne, Gauguin), and more.
✪ See the Orsay Museum Tour on page 69.

▲▲Orangerie Museum (Musée de l'Orangerie)
Step out of the tree-lined, sun-dappled Impressionist painting that is the

Orangerie—Monet's eight monumental canvases immerse you in his garden world of Giverny.

Major Museums Neighborhood

Map labels:

OPERA GARNIER

Opéra · Place de l'Opéra · BD. DES ITALIENS

FAUCHON · HEDIARD

8e

LA MADELEINE

FAUCHON · BLVD. DES CAPUCINES · RUE DE

Place de la Madeleine · BD. DE LA MADELEINE

4 SEPTEMBRE · Quatre Septembre

RUE ST. AUGUSTIN · Bourse

RUE DE LA PAIX · AVE. DE L'OPERA

GALLERIE VIVIENNE · R. VIVIENNE

Madeleine · LADURÉE

RUE CAMBON · RUE DES CAPUCINES

RITZ HOTEL

Place Vendôme

US EMBASSY · RUE ROYALE · RUE ST. FLORENTIN · WH SMITH

RUE DES PETITS CHAMPS

Concorde

AVE. DES CHAMPS-ELYSEES

Place de la Concorde

RUE DE CASTIGLIONE · RUE DE RIVOLI · RUE ST. HONORE · RUE ST. ROCH

Pyramides

RUE DE RICHELIEU

Jardin du Palais Royal

OBELISK · KIDS PLAY AREA · WC

1e

ORANGERIE · Tuileries

Tuileries Garden

RUE DES PYRAMIDES

Place du Palais Royal · PALAIS ROYAL

#69 westbound · Palais Royal–Musée du Louvre · #69 westbound

RUE CROIX DES PETITS CHAMPS

PONT DE LA CONC.

RIVERSIDE PROMENADE · Q. ANATOLE FRANCE

QUAI DES TUILERIES

#69 westbound

ARC DU CARROUSEL

Place du Carrousel

LOUVRE

Louvre-Rivoli

RUE DE L'AMIRAL DE COLIGNY

FRENCH NATIONAL ASSEMBLY

PONT SOLF.

Seine

PONT ROYAL

QUAI FRANCOIS MITTERAND · #69 eastbound

#69 eastbound

Assemblée Nationale · Musée d'Orsay

ORSAY MUSEUM

QUAI VOLTAIRE · QUAI

#69 westbound

To Eiffel Tower · Solférino · RUE DE L'UNIVERSITE · RUE DU BAC · PONT DU CARR.

#69 eastbound

River

PONT DES ARTS

Ile de la Cité

RUE ST. DOMINIQUE

To Rodin Museum & Army Museum

RUE DE BELLECHASSE · ST. GERMAIN

6e

QUAI MALAQUAIS · QUAI DES STS. PERES

#69 westbound

300 Meters

300 Yards

Legend: – – – Madeleine Shopping Walk

Tuileries Garden and into the Orangerie (oh-rahn-zhuh-ree), a little bijou of select works by Claude Monet and his contemporaries. Start with the museum's claim to fame: Monet's *Water Lilies*. These eight mammoth, curved panels immerse you in Monet's garden. Working at his home in Giverny, Monet built a special studio with skylights and wheeled easels to accommodate the canvases. Some call this the first "art installation"—art displayed in a space specially designed to enhance the viewer's experience. We're looking at the pond in his garden at Giverny—dotted with water lilies, surrounded by foliage, and dappled by the reflections of the sky, clouds, and trees on the surface.

Downstairs you'll see artists that bridge the Impressionist and Modernist worlds—Utrillo, Cézanne, Renoir, Matisse, and Picasso. Together they provide a snapshot of what was hot in the world of art collecting, circa 1920.

▶ *€9, €6.50 after 17:00, €16 combo-ticket with Orsay, €18.50 combo-ticket with Monet's Garden and House at Giverny, covered by Museum Pass. Open Wed-Mon 9:00-18:00, closed Tue. Audioguide-€5. English tours usually Mon and Thu at 14:30 and Sat at 11:00. In the Tuileries Garden near Place de la Concorde, Mo: Concorde. Tel. 01 44 77 80 07, www.musee-orangerie.fr.*

EIFFEL TOWER AND NEARBY

From the Eiffel Tower to the golden dome of Invalides, this area has fine museums and the refined ambience of the Rue Cler (served by a number of Métro stops; the RER may be more useful).

▲▲▲Eiffel Tower (La Tour Eiffel)
The 1,063-foot tower was built as a tourist attraction, and it's still the must-see sight in Paris.
✪ See the Eiffel Tower Tour chapter on page 99.

▲Paris Sewer Tour (Les Egouts de Paris)
Discover what happens after you flush. This quick, interesting, and slightly stinky visit takes you along a few hundred yards of water tunnels in the world's first and longest underground sewer system. With good English information, you'll trace the sewer's evolution: from Roman times to medieval (washed straight into the river), to Victor Hugo's fictional hero Jean Valjean (who hid here in *Les Misérables*), to today's 1,500 miles of tunnels carrying 317 million gallons of water daily.

▶ *€4.40, covered by Museum Pass. Open Sat-Wed 11:00-17:00, Oct-April until 16:00, closed Thu-Fri. At the south end of Pont de l'Alma, Mo: Alma-Marceau, RER: Pont de l'Alma. Tel. 01 53 68 27 81.*

▲Riverside Promenade (Les Berges du Seine)
This one-time busy expressway turned popular riverfront park runs along the Left Bank of the Seine from the Pont de l'Alma to the Orsay Museum,

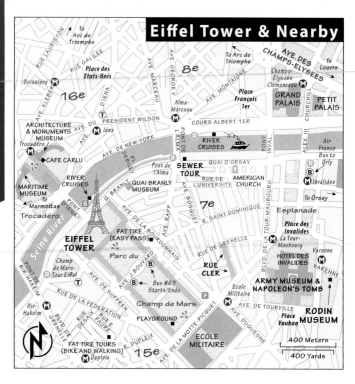

Eiffel Tower & Nearby

allowing walkers to experience the Seine at water level. Distractions abound, with loads of kid-friendly activities, gardens, lively cafés, sling chairs, crêperies, and more.

▲▲Army Museum and Napoleon's Tomb (Musée de l'Armée)

The complex of Les Invalides—a former veterans' hospital built by Louis XIV—has Napoleon's tomb and Europe's greatest military museum. Here you can watch the art of war unfold from stone axes to Axis powers.

At the center of the complex, Napoleon Bonaparte lies majestically dead inside several coffins under a grand dome—a goose-bumping pilgrimage for historians. Your visit continues through an impressive range of museums filled with medieval armor, cannons and muskets, Louis XIV-era uniforms and weapons, and Napoleon's horse—stuffed and mounted.

The best section is dedicated to the two World Wars. Walk chronologically through displays on the trench warfare of World War I, the victory parades, France's horrendous losses, and the humiliating Treaty of Versailles that led to World War II. The WWII rooms use black-and-white photos, maps, videos, and a few artifacts to trace Hitler's rise, the Blitzkrieg that overran France, America's entry into the war, D-Day, the concentration camps, the atomic bomb, the war in the Pacific, and the eventual Allied victory. There's special insight into France's role (the French Resistance), and how it was Charles de Gaulle who actually won the war.

► *€11, €9 after 17:00 (16:00 in Nov-March), covered by Museum Pass, videoguide-€6. Open daily 10:00-18:00, Nov-March until 17:00; tomb also open July-Aug until 19:00 and April-Sept Tue until 21:00; museum (except for tomb) closed first Mon of month Oct-June; Charles de Gaulle exhibit closed Mon year-round. 129 Rue de Grenelle, Mo: La Tour Maubourg, Varenne, or Invalides. Tel. 08 10 11 33 99, www.musee-armee.fr.*

Sights

▲▲Rodin Museum (Musée Rodin)

This recently renovated, user-friendly museum is filled with passionate works by the greatest sculptor since Michelangelo, well-displayed in the mansion where the sculptor Auguste Rodin lived and worked, You'll see *The Kiss, The Thinker, The Gates of Hell,* and many more.

Rodin sculpted human figures on an epic scale, revealing through their bodies his deepest thoughts and feelings. Like many of Michelangelo's unfinished works, Rodin's statues rise from the raw stone around them,

Rodin Museum—*The Kiss, The Thinker,* and more

The Army Museum's WWII wing

driven by the life force. With missing limbs and scarred skin, these are prefab classics, making ugliness noble. Rodin's people are always moving restlessly. Even the famous *Thinker* is moving; while he's plopped down solidly, his mind is a million miles away.

Exhibits trace Rodin's artistic development, explain how his bronze statues were cast, and show the studies he created to work up to his masterpiece, the unfinished *Gates of Hell*. Learn about Rodin's tumultuous relationship with his apprentice and lover, Camille Claudel. Mull over what makes his sculptures some of the most evocative since the Renaissance. And stroll the beautiful gardens, packed with many of his greatest works and ideal for artistic reflection.

▶ *€10, free on first Sun of the month, €4 for just the garden, €18 combo-ticket with Orsay, covered by Museum Pass. Open Tue-Sun 10:00-17:45, closed Mon; gardens close at 18:00, Oct-March at 17:00. Audioguide-€6, mandatory baggage check. Near the golden dome of Invalides at 77 Rue de Varenne, Mo: Varenne. Tel. 01 44 18 61 10, www. musee-rodin.fr.*

▲▲Marmottan Museum (Musée Marmottan Monet)

This intimate, untouristy mansion on the southwest fringe of urban Paris has the best collection of works by the father of Impressionism, Claude Monet. Fiercely independent and dedicated to his craft, Monet gave courage to the other Impressionists in the face of harsh criticism.

Though the museum is not arranged chronologically, you can trace his life. You'll see black-and-white sketches from his youth, his discovery of open-air painting, and the canvas—*Impression: Sunrise*—that gave Impressionism its name. There are portraits of his wives and kids, and his well-known "series" paintings (done at different times of day) of London, Gare St. Lazare, and the Cathedral of Rouen. The museum's highlight is scenes from his garden at Giverny—the rose trellis, the Japanese bridge, and the larger-than-life water lilies.

In addition, the Marmottan features a world-class collection of works by Berthe Morisot and other Impressionists and an eclectic collection of non-Monet objects, such as furniture and illuminated manuscript drawings.

▶ *€11, not covered by Museum Pass. Open Tue-Sun 10:00-18:00, Thu until 21:00, closed Mon. Audioguide-€3. 2 Rue Louis-Boilly, Mo: La Muette. Tel. 01 44 96 50 33, www.marmottan.fr.*

Best Views Over the City of Light

Eiffel Tower: The ultimate. Period.
Paris Ferris Wheel: Offers a 200-foot-high view of Paris.
Arc de Triomphe: Best at night when the Champs-Elysées positively glitters.
Notre-Dame's Tower: In the heart of Paris, among the gargoyles.
Steps of Sacré-Cœur: Join the guitar-strumming partiers on Paris' only hilltop.
Galeries Lafayette or Printemps: Both department stores have a stunning overlook of the old Opéra district.
Montparnasse Tower: This lone skyscraper's views are best by day.
Pompidou Center: Great views plus exciting modern art.
Place du Trocadéro: It's at street level, but is the best place to see the Eiffel Tower.
Bar at Hôtel Hyatt-Regency: Bar on 34th floor with a stunning night-time panorama.

LEFT BANK

The Left Bank is as much an attitude as an actual neighborhood. There are fewer busy boulevards, businessmen in suits, and modern buildings, and more quiet lanes, students, and intimate cafés. The sightseeing core stretches roughly from the Panthéon to St. Germain-des-Prés, and from the river to Luxembourg Garden.

The part of the Left Bank called the **Latin Quarter** is immediately across the river from Notre-Dame. This was medieval Paris' university district, where scholars spoke Latin. The neighborhood's main boulevards (St. Michel and St. Germain) are lined with cafés—once the haunts of great poets and philosophers, now the hangouts of tired tourists. Though still youthful and artsy, much of this area has become a tourist ghetto. Exploring a few blocks up or downriver from here gives you a better feeling for what survives of Paris' classic Left Bank.

Lively nighttime hotspots on the Left Bank include areas around St. Germain-des-Prés Church, Rue de Buci, Rue des Canettes (near St.

Sulpice), and the Latin Quarter. ✪ For boutique shopping, follow the route shown on the map below.

▲▲Cluny Museum (Musée National du Moyen Age)

The Cluny is a treasure trove of Middle Ages (Moyen Age) art. Located within a Roman bathhouse, it offers close-up looks at stained glass, Notre-Dame carvings, fine goldsmithing and jewelry, and rooms of tapestries. The highlights are several original stained-glass windows from Sainte-Chapelle and the exquisite series of six Lady and the Unicorn tapestries: A delicate, as-medieval-as-can-be noble lady introduces a delighted unicorn to the senses of taste, hearing, sight, smell, and touch. The sixth is the most talked-about tapestry: *A Mon Seul Désir (To My Sole Desire)*. What is the lady's only desire? Is it that jewel box, or is it something—or

someone—inside that tent? Human sensuality is awakening, an old dark age is ending, and the Renaissance is emerging.

▶ *€8, includes audioguide, free on first Sun of month, covered by Museum Pass (pass holders pay €1 for audioguide). Open Wed-Mon 9:15-17:45, closed Tue. Located at 6 Place Paul Painlevé, Mo: Cluny-La Sorbonne, St. Michel, or Odéon. Tel. 01 53 73 78 16, www.musee-moyenage.fr.*

▲St. Sulpice Church

For pipe-organ enthusiasts, a visit here is one of Europe's great musical treats. The Grand Orgue at St. Sulpice Church has a rich history, with a succession of 12 world-class organists that goes back 300 years. Patterned after St. Paul's Cathedral in London, the church has a Neoclassical arcaded facade and two round towers. Inside, in the first chapel on the right, are three murals of fighting angels by Delacroix. The fourth chapel on the right has a statue of Joan of Arc and wall plaques listing hundreds from St. Sulpice's congregation who died during World War I. The north transept wall features an Egyptian-style obelisk used as a gnomon on a sundial. The last chapel before the exit has a display on the Shroud of Turin.

You can hear the organ play at Sunday Mass (10:30-11:30, dress appropriately), followed by a high-powered 25-minute recital, usually performed by talented organist Daniel Roth.

▶ *Free, open daily 7:30-19:30, Mo: St. Sulpice or Mabillon. See www.stsulpice.com for special concerts.*

▲Luxembourg Garden (Jardin du Luxembourg)

This lovely 60-acre garden is an Impressionist painting brought to life. Slip into a green chair pondside, enjoy the radiant flower beds, go jogging,

Head to the Cluny Museum for medieval art.

Luxembourg Garden—an urban oasis

play tennis or basketball, sail a toy sailboat, or take in a chess game or puppet show (Les Guignols, like Punch and Judy). The garden, dotted with fountains and statues, is the property of the French Senate, which meets here in the Luxembourg Palace. There's no better place to watch Parisians at play.

▶ *Open daily dawn until dusk, Mo: Odéon, RER: Luxembourg.*

▲Panthéon

This state-capitol-style Neoclassical monument celebrates France's illustrious history and people, balances a Foucault pendulum, and is the final home of many French VIPs.

Inside the vast, evenly lit space—360 feet long, 280 feet wide, and 270 feet high—monuments trace the celebrated struggles of the French people: a beheaded St. Denis (painting on left wall of nave), St. Geneviève saving the fledgling city from Attila the Hun, and scenes of Joan of Arc (left transept). A Foucault pendulum swings gracefully at the end of a cable suspended from the towering dome. It was here in 1851 that the scientist Léon Foucault first demonstrated the rotation of the earth. A panoply of greats are buried in the crypt: Rousseau, Voltaire, Victor Hugo, Alexandre Dumas, Louis Braille, and Marie Curie. It's 206 steps to the base of the dome, with views of the interior and city.

▶ *€8.50, covered by Museum Pass, €2 for dome climb (not covered by Museum Pass). Open daily 10:00-18:30, Oct-March until 18:00, last entry 45 minutes before closing. Audioguide-€5. Escorted dome visits leave hourly. Mo: Cardinal Lemoine. Tel. 01 44 32 18 00, http://pantheon.monuments-nationaux.fr.*

Montparnasse Tower (La Tour Montparnasse)

This sadly out-of-place 59-story superscraper has one virtue: If you can't make it up the Eiffel Tower, the sensational views from this tower are cheaper, far easier to access, and make for a fair consolation prize. Come early in the day for clearest skies and shortest lines, and be treated to views from a comfortable interior and from up on the rooftop. Sunset is great but views are disappointing after dark.

▶ *€16, 30 percent discount with this book, not covered by Museum Pass. Open daily 9:30-23:30, Oct-March until 22:30. Enter on Rue de l'Arrivée, Mo: Montparnasse-Bienvenüe (follow sparse Tour signs to exit #4). Tel. 01 45 38 52 56, www.tourmontparnasse56.com.*

▲Catacombs

In 1786, health-conscious Parisians looking to relieve congestion and improve the city's sanitary conditions emptied the church cemeteries and moved the bones here, to former limestone quarries. Your visit covers a one-mile, one-hour route through tunnels containing the anonymous bones of six million permanent Parisians. The bones are stacked in piles five feet high and as much as 80 feet deep.

Descend 60 feet (130 steps) below street level and ponder the sign announcing, "Halt, this is the empire of the dead." Shuffle through passageways of skull-studded tibiae and past more cheery signs: "Happy is he who is forever faced with the hour of his death and prepares himself for the end every day." Then climb 86 steps to emerge far from where you entered, with white-limestone-covered toes, telling everyone you've been underground gawking at bones. Note to wannabe Hamlets: An attendant checks your bag at the exit for stolen souvenirs.

▶ *€12, advance tickets available, not covered by Museum Pass. Open Tue-Sun 10:00-20:30, closed Mon. Lines can be long between 10:00 and 16:00—arrive by 9:30 to minimize the wait; come no later than 19:00 or risk not getting in. Audioguide-€5. Enter at 1 Place Denfert-Rochereau, Mo: Denfert-Rochereau. You'll exit after your visit at 36 Rue Remy Dumoncel; turn right and walk several blocks to either Mo: Alésia or Mouton Duvernet. Tel. 01 43 22 47 63, www.catacombs.paris.fr.*

CHAMPS-ELYSEES AND NEARBY

This famous boulevard is Paris' backbone, stretching from the Arc de Triomphe downhill to Place de la Concorde. This is Paris at its most Parisian: monumental sidewalks, stylish shops, elegant cafés, glimmering showrooms, and proud Parisians on parade.

▲▲▲Champs-Elysées

Though the Champs-Elysées has become as international as it is Parisian, a walk down the two-mile boulevard is still a must. It's a great walk by day, and even better at night, allowing you to tap into the city's increasingly global scene.

In 1667, Louis XIV opened the first section of the street, and it soon became *the* place to cruise in your carriage. (It still is today.) By the 1920s,

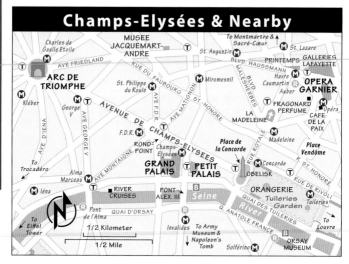

Champs-Elysées & Nearby

this boulevard was pure elegance—fancy residences, rich hotels, and cafés. Today it's home to big business, celebrity cafés, glitzy nightclubs, high-fashion shopping, and international people-watching. People gather here to celebrate Bastille Day (July 14), World Cup triumphs, and the finale of the Tour de France.

Start at the Arc de Triomphe (Mo: Charles de Gaulle-Etoile) and head downhill on the left-hand side. The arrival of McDonald's (at #140) was an unthinkable horror, but these days dining *chez MacDo* has become typically Parisian, and this branch is the most profitable one in the world.

Fancy car showrooms abound, including Peugeot (#136). The Lido (#116) is Paris' largest burlesque-type cabaret (and a multiplex cinema). Across the boulevard is the flagship store of leather-bag makers Louis Vuitton (#101). Fouquet's café (#99) is a popular spot for French celebrities, especially movie stars—note the names in the sidewalk in front. Enter if you dare for a €10 espresso. Ladurée café (#75) is also classy but has a welcoming and affordable take-out bakery.

Continuing on, you pass international-brand stores, such as Sephora, Nike, Disney, and the Gap. You can end your walk at the round Rond Point intersection (Mo: Franklin D. Roosevelt) or continue to obelisk-studded Place de la Concorde, Paris' largest square.

▲▲Arc de Triomphe

Napoleon had the magnificent Arc de Triomphe commissioned to commemorate his victory at the 1805 battle of Austerlitz. The foot of the arch is a stage on which the last two centuries of Parisian history have played out—from the funeral of Napoleon to the goose-stepping arrival of the Nazis to the triumphant return of Charles de Gaulle after the Allied liberation. Examine the carvings on the pillars, featuring a mighty Napoleon and excitable Lady Liberty. Pay your respects at the Tomb of the Unknown Soldier where, every day at 18:30, the flame is rekindled and new flowers set in place.

Now climb the 284 steps to the observation deck up top, with sweeping skyline panoramas and a mesmerizing view down onto the traffic that swirls around the arch. You're at the center of a grand axis of city planning, stretching from the Louvre, up the Champs-Elysées to the Arc de Triomphe, then continuing west to the huge rectangular, modern Grande Arche de la Défense. Looking down you see 12 converging boulevards forming a star *(étoile)*. What a traffic mess! Or is it? Cars entering the circle have the right of way; those in the circle must yield.

▶ *€9.50 to climb, free on first Sun of month Oct-March, covered by Museum Pass. Open daily 10:00-23:00, Oct-March until 22:30, last entry 45 minutes before closing. Use the underpass to reach the arch. Mo: Charles de Gaulle-Etoile. Tel. 01 55 37 73 77, www.paris-arc-de-triomphe.fr.*

Champs-Elysées with Arc de Triomphe

Opéra Garnier's grand staircase

▲Petit Palais (and its Musée des Beaux-Arts)

This free museum displays a broad collection of paintings and sculpture from the 1600s to the 1900s on its ground floor, and an easy-to-appreciate collection of art from Greek antiquities to Art Nouveau in its basement. There are a few diamonds in the rough, including Courbet's soft-porn *The Sleepers* (*Le Sommeil,* 1866), capturing two women nestled in post-climactic bliss; Monet's hazy, moody *Sunset on the Seine at Lavacourt* (1880), painted the winter after his wife died; and works by the American painter Mary Cassatt and other Impressionists.

▶ *Free. Open Tue-Sun 10:00-18:00, Fri until 21:00 for special exhibits, closed Mon. Audioguide-€5. On Avenue Winston Churchill, Mo: Champs-Elysées-Clemenceau. Tel. 01 53 43 40 00, www.petitpalais.paris.fr.*

▲Paris Ferris Wheel (Roue de Paris)

The Paris Ferris Wheel, situated on Place de la Concorde or in the Tuileries Garden, offers a 200-foot-high view of Paris. Your ticket covers two slow revolutions, and generally it's two passengers per gondola.

▶ *€12, open long hours daily in high season.*

OPERA NEIGHBORHOOD

▲▲Opéra Garnier

A gleaming grand theater of the belle époque, the Palais Garnier was built for Napoleon III and finished in 1875. For the best exterior view, stand in front of the Opéra Métro stop. The building is huge. Its massive foundations straddle an underground lake (inspiring the mysterious world of *The Phantom of the Opera*). It's the masterpiece of architect Charles Garnier, who oversaw every element, from laying the foundations to what color the wallpaper should be.

To see the interior, you can take a guided tour (your best look), tour the public areas on your own (using the audioguide), or attend a performance. The building is huge, though the auditorium itself seats only 2,000 (note that the auditorium is sometimes off-limits due to performances and rehearsals). There's a cavernous backstage to accommodate elaborate sets, as well as the extravagant lobbies out front. That's where the real show took place, between acts, when the elite of Paris—out to see and be seen—strutted their elegant stuff.

Visitors can explore the lobbies, the grand marble staircase, and the Grand Foyer, a long, high-ceilinged Hall-of-Mirrors-esque space. The small museum will interest opera buffs. The highlight of the visit is a view from the upper seats into the actual red-velvet performance hall. There you can see Marc Chagall's colorful ceiling (1964) and a seven-ton chandelier.

Near the Opéra are the Fragonard Perfume Museum (free, 9 Rue Scribe), the venerable Galeries Lafayette department store, and the glitterati-flecked Café de la Paix (12 Boulevard des Capucines).

▸ *€11, not covered by Museum Pass. Generally open daily 10:00-16:30, mid-July-Aug until 18:00. Audioguide-€5. Guided English tours at 11:30 and 14:30 July-Aug daily, Sept-June Wed, Sat, and Sun only—call to confirm (€14.50, 1.5 hours, tel. 01 40 01 17 89 or 08 25 05 44 05). 8 Rue Scribe, Mo: Opéra.*

For performances, check the schedule and buy tickets at the ticket office (open Mon-Sat 11:30-18:30 and an hour before the show, closed Sun) or online (www.operadeparis.fr).

▲▲Jacquemart-André Museum (Musée Jacquemart-André)

This thoroughly enjoyable museum-mansion showcases the lavish home of a wealthy, art-loving, 19th-century Parisian couple. Edouard André and his wife Nélie Jacquemart—who had no children—spent their lives and fortunes designing, building, and then decorating this sumptuous mansion. The place is strewn with paintings by Rembrandt, Botticelli, Uccello, Mantegna, Bellini, Boucher, and Fragonard. Though there are no must-see masterpieces, the art gathered here would still be enough to make any gallery famous.

The museum's sumptuous tearoom serves delicious cakes and tea. A few blocks north is Paris' most beautiful park, Parc Monceau.

▸ *€12, includes excellent audioguide, not covered by Museum Pass. Open daily 10:00-18:00, Mon until 20:30 during special exhibits (which are common). 158 Boulevard Haussmann, Mo: St. Philippe-du-Roule. Tel. 01 45 62 11 59, www.musee-jacquemart-andre.com.*

MARAIS NEIGHBORHOOD AND MORE

The Marais extends along the Right Bank of the Seine, from the Bastille to the Pompidou Center. The main west–east axis is formed by Rue St.

Antoine, Rue des Rosiers (the heart of Paris' Jewish community), and Rue Ste. Croix de la Bretonnerie. The centerpiece of the neighborhood is the stately Place des Vosges. Don't waste time looking for the Bastille, the prison of Revolution fame. It's Paris' most famous non-sight. The building is long gone, and just the square remains. Mo: Bastille, St-Paul, and Hôtel de Ville.

▲Strolling the Marais

With more pre-Revolutionary lanes and mansions than anywhere else in town, the Marais is more atmospheric than touristy. In the 1600s, this former swamp (marais) became home to artistocrats' private mansions (hôtels), located close to the king's townhouse on stylish Place des Vosges. With the Revolution, the Marais turned working-class, filled with artisans and immigrants, and became home to Paris' Jewish community. Today the area is trending upward and becoming home to young professionals.

For a good east-to-west introductory walk, start at Place de la Bastille (nightlife) and head west on busy Rue Saint-Antoine to Place des Vosges (art galleries, restaurants). Continue west on Rue des Francs-Bourgeois (fashion boutiques), turning onto Rue des Rosiers (Jewish neighborhood) and Rue Ste. Croix de la Bretonnerie (gay Paree's LGBT community). On Sunday afternoons, the area pulses with shoppers and café crowds.

▲Place des Vosges

Henry IV built this centerpiece of the Marais in 1605 and called it "Place Royale." As he'd hoped, it turned the Marais into Paris' most exclusive neighborhood. In the center, a statue of Louis XIII, on horseback, gestures, "Look at this wonderful square my dad built." He's surrounded by locals enjoying their community park, children frolicking in the sandbox, lovers warming benches, and pigeons guarding their fountains while trees shade this escape from the glare of the big city. Around the square, arcades shade cafés and art galleries.

Study the architecture: nine pavilions (houses) per side. The two highest—at the front and back—were for the king and queen (but were never used). Warm red brickwork—some real, some fake—is topped with sloped slate roofs, chimneys, and another quaint relic of a bygone era: TV antennas.

At 6 Place des Vosges is **Victor Hugo's House,** a free museum dedicated to France's literary giant (at the southeast corner of the square,

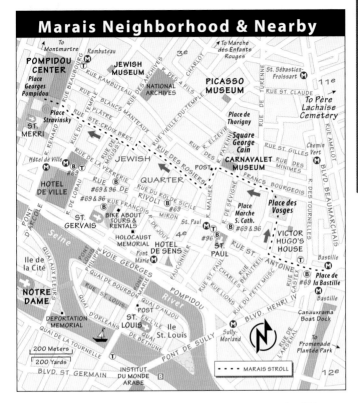

marked by the French flag). This was where he wrote much of his most important work, including *Les Misérables* (open Tue-Sun 10:00-18:00, closed Mon).

▲Carnavalet Museum (Musée Carnavalet)

The tumultuous history of Paris—starring the Revolutionary years—is well portrayed in this converted Marais mansion (at 23 Rue de Sévigné, closed for renovation throughout 2017 and beyond). The museum contains models of medieval Paris, maps of the city over the centuries, paintings of Parisian scenes, French Revolution paraphernalia—including a small guillotine—and fully furnished rooms re-creating life in Paris in different eras.

▲▲▲Picasso Museum (Musée Picasso)

The 20th century's most famous and—OK, I'll say it—greatest artist was the master of many styles (Cubism, Surrealism, Expressionism, etc.) and of many media (painting, sculpture, prints, ceramics, and assemblages). Still, he could make anything he touched look unmistakably like "a Picasso."

The Picasso Museum has the world's largest collection of his work—some 400 paintings, sculptures, sketches, and ceramics—spread across five levels of this mansion in the Marais. A visit here walks you through the full range of this complex man's life and art. The core of the museum is organized chronologically.

Born in Spain, Picasso (1881-1973) was the son of an art teacher. In 1900, the brash Spaniard moved to Paris, the undisputed world capital of culture. Poor and homesick, he entered his "Blue Period," painting emaciated beggars, hard-eyed pimps, and himself, bundled up against the cold.

In 1904, Picasso moved into his Bateau-Lavoir studio on Montmartre, got a steady girlfriend, and suddenly saw the world through rose-colored glasses—the Rose Period. With his neighbor, Georges Braque, Picasso invented Cubism, fracturing a figure into a barely recognizable jumble of "cube"-like facets. In a few short years, Picasso had turned painting in the direction it would go for the next 50 years.

After World War I, Picasso moved to the Montparnasse neighborhood, immersing himself in Paris' rich cultural life. In 1940, Nazi tanks rolled into Paris. Picasso's war-era paintings are gray and bleak.

At war's end, Picasso left Paris for the sunny skies of the French Riviera. He was reborn, enjoying worldwide fame and the love of a woman a third his age (Picasso had a number of wives/girlfriends/muses over the years—the museum has several of their portraits). Picasso's Riviera works are bright, lighthearted, and childlike, featuring new media (especially pottery) and motifs of the sea. He was fertile to the end, still painting with bright thick colors at age 91.

▶ *€11, covered by Museum Pass, free on first Sun of month. Open Tue-Fri 10:30-18:00, Sat-Sun 9:30-18:00, closed Mon, last entry 45 minutes before closing. Videoguide-€4. Timed-entry tickets available on* *museum website but lines generally aren't bad. 5 Rue de Thorigny, Mo: St. Sébastien-Froissart, St. Paul, or Chemin Vert. Tel. 01 42 71 25 21, www.musee-picasso.fr.*

▲Rue des Rosiers: Paris' Jewish Quarter

The intersection of Rue des Rosiers and Rue des Ecouffes marks the heart of the small neighborhood that Jews call the Pletzl ("little square"). Once the largest in Western Europe, Paris' Jewish Quarter is much smaller today but still colorful. Lively Rue des Ecouffes, named for a bird of prey, is a derogatory nod to the moneychangers' shops that once lined this lane. The next two blocks along Rue des Rosiers feature kosher *(cascher)* restaurants and fast-food places selling falafel, *shawarma, kefta,* and other Mediterranean dishes. Bakeries specialize in braided challah, bagels, and strudels. Delis offer gefilte fish, piroshkis, and blintzes. Art galleries exhibit Jewish-themed works, and store windows post flyers for community events. Need a menorah? You'll find one here.

▲Jewish Art and History Museum (Musée d'Art et Histoire du Judaïsme)

This is a fine museum of historical artifacts and rare ritual objects spanning the Jewish people's long cultural heritage. It emphasizes the cultural unity maintained by this continually dispersed population. You'll learn about Jewish traditions, and see exquisite costumes and objects central to daily life and religious practices. Those with a background in Judaism or who take the time with the thoughtful audioguide and information (some but not all posted info is in English) will be rewarded.

▶ *€9, includes audioguide, covered by Museum Pass. Open Tue-Fri 11:00-18:00, Sat-Sun 10:00-18:00, open later during special exhibits—Wed*

Rue des Rosiers draws Jewish shoppers.

Pompidou—wild and crazy modern art

until 21:00 and Sat-Sun until 19:00, closed Mon, last entry 45 minutes before closing. 71 Rue du Temple, Mo: Rambuteau or Hôtel de Ville. Tel. 01 53 01 86 60, www.mahj.org.

▲▲Pompidou Center (Centre Pompidou)

Some people hate modern art. But the Pompidou Center contains what is possibly Europe's best collection of 20th-century art. In addition, the occasional temporary exhibitions, the great rooftop view, and the perpetual street fair of performers and crêpe stands outside all make this museum worthwhile.

The colorful building is exoskeletal (like a crab or Notre-Dame), with its functional parts—the pipes, heating ducts, and escalator—on the outside, and the meaty art inside. It's the epitome of modern architecture, where "form follows function."

The permanent collection (on the fourth and fifth floors) features all the big names of the early 20th century—Matisse, Picasso, Chagall, Dalí—and continues with contemporary art. This art was ahead of its time and is still waiting for the world to catch up. After so many Madonnas-and-children, a piano smashed to bits and glued to the wall is refreshing. Once you've seen the permanent collection, explore the temporary exhibits to connect with what is "now" from around the globe.

▸ *€14, free on first Sun of month, €3 for View of Paris ticket. The Museum Pass covers the permanent collection and escalators to sixth-floor panoramic views (plus occasional special exhibits). Open Wed-Mon 11:00-21:00, closed Tue, ticket counters close at 20:00. Mo: Rambuteau or Hôtel de Ville. Tel. 01 44 78 12 33, www.centrepompidou.fr.*

▲Père Lachaise Cemetery (Cimetière du Père Lachaise)

Littered with the tombstones of many of the city's most illustrious dead, this is your best one-stop look at Paris' fascinating, romantic past residents. More like a small city, the cemetery is big and confusing. Buy grave-locator maps from nearby florists or street vendors to locate the graves of Frédéric Chopin (the Polish pianist whose tomb always sports fresh flowers), Molière (playwright to Louis XIV), Edith Piaf (warbling singer who regretted nothing), Oscar Wilde (controversial figure who died in Paris), Jim Morrison (ditto), Gertrude Stein (American writer), Héloïse and Abélard (illicit medieval lovers), and many more.

▶ *Free. Open Mon-Fri 8:00-18:00, Sat 8:30-18:00, Sun 9:00-18:00, until 17:30 in winter. The best entrance is Porte Gambetta, two blocks from Mo: Gambetta (do not go to Mo: Père Lachaise) and bus #69's last stop. Tel. 01 55 25 82 10, map available at unofficial website: www. pere-lachaise.com.*

▲▲Sacré-Cœur and Montmartre

Montmarte, Paris' highest hill, is topped by Sacré-Cœur Basilica and is best known as the home of cabaret nightlife and bohemian artists. Struggling painters, poets, dreamers, and drunkards came here for cheap rent, untaxed booze, rustic landscapes, and views of the underwear of high-kicking cancan girls at the Moulin Rouge. These days, the hill is equal parts charm and kitsch—still vaguely village-like but mobbed with tourists and pickpockets on sunny weekends. Come for a bit of history, a getaway from Paris' noisy boulevards, and the view (to beat the crowds, it's best on a weekday or early on weekend mornings).

Start your visit at the **Sacré-Cœur** (Sacred Heart) Basilica. The striking exterior, with its onion domes and bleached-bone pallor, looks ancient, but it was finished only a century ago. Inside, you'll see impressive mosaics (including one of Jesus with his sacred heart burning with love and compassion for humanity), a statue of St. Thérèse, a scale model of the church, and three stained-glass windows dedicated to Joan of Arc. For an unobstructed panoramic view of Paris, climb 260 feet (300 steps) up the tight and claustrophobic spiral stairs to the top of the dome (church is free, open daily 6:00-22:30; dome costs €6, not covered by Museum Pass, open daily May-Sept 9:30-19:00, Oct-April until 17:00; tel 01 53 41 89 00, www.sacre-coeur-montmartre.com).

Chopin's grave at Père Lachaise Cemetery

Montmartre, capped with Sacré-Cœur

Montmartre's main square, **Place du Tertre,** one block from the church, was once the haunt of Henri de Toulouse-Lautrec and the original bohemians. Today, it's crawling with tourists and unoriginal bohemians (to beat the crowds, it's best on a weekday or early on weekend mornings).

The **Montmartre Museum** re-creates the traditional cancan-and-cabaret Montmartre scene, with paintings, posters, photos, music, and memorabilia, and offers a chance to see the studio of Maurice Utrillo (€9.50, includes audioguide, not covered by Museum Pass, open daily 10:00-18:00, Aug-Sept until 19:00, last entry 45 minutes before closing, 12 Rue Cortot, tel. 01 49 25 89 39, www.museedemontmartre.fr).

A few blocks away are the historic Au Lapin Agile cabaret (still in business) and the Moulin de la Galette, a dance hall featured in a famous Renoir painting (✪ see page 86). Wandering the neighborhood, you can see the (boring) exteriors of former homes of Picasso, Toulouse-Lautrec, Van Gogh, and composer Erik Satie.

At the base of the hill (near Mo: Blanche), the Moulin Rouge ("Red Windmill") nightclub still offers glitzy, pricey shows to busloads of tourists. The neighborhood around it, called Pigalle, is pretty rough and raunchy, with sex shops and bars where a €150 bottle of cheap champagne comes with a friend.

▸ *To reach Montmartre, take the Métro to the Anvers stop (to avoid the stairs up to Sacré-Cœur, buy one more Métro ticket and ride up on the funicular). Or from Place Pigalle, take the "Montmartrobus," which drops you right by Sacré-Cœur (Funiculaire stop, costs one Métro ticket, 4/hour). A taxi from the Seine or the Bastille is about €15 (€20 at night).*

DAY TRIPS FROM PARIS

▲▲▲Versailles
Twelve miles southwest of Paris, the jaw-dropping residence of French kings features a lavish palace and expansive, fountain-dotted gardens.
▸ ✪ *See the Versailles Tour chapter on page 121.*

▲▲Chartres: The Town and the Cathedral
One of Europe's greatest Gothic cathedrals soars above the pleasant town of Chartres, an hour southwest of Paris.

A Page of History

The Beginnings (A.D.1-1500): Julius Caesar conquered the Parisii, turning Paris from a tribal fishing village into a European city. The mix of Latin (southern) and Celtic (northern) cultures, with Paris right in the middle, defined the French character. Roman Paris fell to the Franks (hence "France") and Norsemen ("Normans"). Charlemagne (768-814) briefly united the Franks, giving a glimpse of modern France.

In 1066, William the Conqueror awkwardly united England and France, bringing centuries of border wars. Eventually, the teenage visionary Joan of Arc (1412-1431) rallied the French to drive the English out. Modern France was born.

France Dominates (1500-1789): Renaissance kings François I and Henry IV established France as a European power, and Louis XIV made it a superpower. Under Louis XV and XVI, every educated European spoke French and followed French aristocratic customs. Meanwhile, enlightened French philosophers sowed the seeds of democracy.

Revolution (1789-1800): On July 14, 1789, Parisian revolutionaries stormed the Bastille, and eventually beheaded the king and queen. Thousands were guillotined if suspected of hindering democracy's march. From the chaos rose a charismatic commoner: Napoleon Bonaparte.

Elected Emperors and Constitutional Kings (1800s): Napoleon conquered Europe, crowned himself emperor, and invaded Russia, before being defeated at Waterloo. The monarchy was restored, but rulers had to toe the democratic line. Eventually, Napoleon's nephew (Napoleon III) presided over a wealthy-but-declining era of big monuments and Impressionist art, known as the belle époque—the "beautiful age."

War and Depression (1900-1950): Two world wars with Germany wasted the country. France lost millions of men in World War I and was easily overrun by Hitler in World War II. Paris, now dirt cheap, attracted foreign writers (Hemingway) and artists (Picasso).

Postwar France (1950-Present): France recovered slowly under wartime hero Charles de Gaulle. As its colonial empire dissolved after bitter wars in Algeria and Vietnam, immigrants flooded Paris. The turbulent '60s, progressive '70s, socialist-turned-conservative '80s, and the middle-of-the-road '90s brought us to the 21st century. Paris has regained its place as one of the world's great cities.

Claude Monet's iconic garden and pond at Giverny

▸ *Catch the train from Paris' Gare Montparnasse (14/day, about €16 one-way). The church is free and open daily 8:30-19:30.*

▲Giverny
Claude Monet's garden still looks like it did when he painted it. Wander among the flowers, the rose trellis, the Japanese Bridge, and the pond filled with lily pads.

▸ *Big bus tours are the easiest way to get there (about €70). On your own, drive or take the Rouen-bound train from Gare St. Lazare to Vernon (8/day Mon-Sat, 6/day Sun, about €30 round-trip, 45 minutes). From Vernon, take the public bus (meets every train, €8 round-trip), a taxi (€15), or rent a bike at the café opposite the train station (€14). Monet's Garden and House are open daily April-Oct 9:30-18:00, closed Nov-March (€9.50, not covered by Museum Pass, tel. 02 32 51 90 31, http:// fondation-monet.com).*

Sleeping

In Paris, choosing the right neighborhood is as important as choosing the right hotel. I've focused most of my recommendations in three safe, handy, and colorful neighborhoods: the village-like Rue Cler (near the Eiffel Tower), the artsy and trendy Marais (near Place de la Bastille), and the lively yet classy Luxembourg (on the Left Bank). I also list places in several other areas: Ile St. Louis, Rue Mouffetard, and Montmartre. I like hotels that are clean, central, relatively quiet at night, reasonably priced, friendly, run with a respect for French traditions, and small enough to have a hands-on owner or manager and stable staff.

Double rooms listed in this book average around €120-180 (with private bathrooms). They range from a low of roughly €60 (very simple, with toilet and shower down the hall) to €400 (maximum plumbing and more).

A Typical Parisian Hotel Room

A typical €150 double room in Paris will be small by American standards. It will have one double bed (either queen-sized or slightly narrower) or two twins. There's probably a bathroom in the room with a toilet, sink, and bathtub or shower. The room has a telephone and TV, and may have a safe. Most hotels at this price will have air-conditioning—cheaper places may not. Single rooms, triples, and quads will have similar features.

Most hotels offer some kind of breakfast, but it's rarely included in the room rates. It's normally a self-service buffet of cereal, cheese, yogurt, fruit, and juice, while a server takes your coffee order.

Hotels have Internet access, either Wi-Fi or a computer in the lobby. Though there may be a charge, at least one of these options is generally free. The staff speaks at least enough English to get by. Night clerks aren't paid enough to care deeply about problems that arise.

Note that the French hotel rating system (zero to five stars) only reflects the number of amenities (e.g., fancier lobbies, more elaborately designed rooms), and does not necessarily rate quality. I rarely pay attention to it when choosing a hotel.

Making Reservations

Reserve months in advance, or as soon as you've pinned down your travel dates, particularly if traveling during peak season (April-Oct, especially May, June, Sept, and Oct) or for a major holiday. Do it by phone, through the hotel's website, or with an email that reads something like this:

Dear Hotel Magnifique,

I would like to reserve a double room for 2 people for 3 nights, arriving 19 July and departing 22 July. If possible, I would like a quiet room with a double bed (not twin beds), air-conditioning, and a shower (not a tub). Please let me know if you have a room available and the price. Thank you.

If they require your credit-card number for a deposit, you can send it by email (I do), but it's safer via a phone call or fax. Once your room is booked, print out the confirmation, and reconfirm your reservation with a phone call or email a day or two in advance (alert them if you'll be arriving after 17:00). If canceling a reservation, some hotels require advance notice—otherwise they may bill you. Even if there's no penalty, it's polite to give at least three days' notice.

Hotel Price Code

$$$$	**Splurge:** Most rooms over €200
$$$	**Pricier:** €150-200
$$	**Moderate:** €100-150
$	**Budget:** €50-100
¢	**Hostel/Backpacker:** Under €50
RS%	**Rick Steves discount**

These rates are for a standard double room without breakfast in high season. For the best prices, book direct.

Budget Tips

To get the best rates, book directly with the hotel, not through a hotel-booking engine. Start with the hotel's website, looking for promo deals. Check rates every few days, as prices can vary greatly based on demand. Email several hotels to ask for their best price and compare offers—you may be astonished at the range. Some of my listed hotels offer a "Rick Steves discount" for readers of this book—it's worth asking when you reserve. Hotels farther from the Seine are cheaper (but less atmospheric or convenient).

Besides hotels, there are cheaper alternatives. I list a few all-ages hostels, which offer €25-35 dorm beds (and a few inexpensive doubles) and come with curfews and other rules. Bed-and-breakfasts (B&Bs) offer a personal touch at a fair price—try www.bed-and-breakfast-in-paris.com. Airbnb.com lets you browse properties and correspond directly with European property owners or managers.

Renting an apartment can save money if you're traveling as a family, staying more than a week, and planning to cook your own meals. Try www.parisperfect.com or www.parisforrent.com (specializing in top-end apartments), www.haveninparis.com (stylish havens for travelers), www.cobblestoneparis.com (furnished rentals with English-speaking greeters), www.francehomestyle.com (personalized service), www.homerental.fr (no agency fees), or www.vrbo.com (putting you directly in touch with owners).

Don't be too cheap when picking a place to stay. Choose a nice, central neighborhood. In summer, pay a little more for air-conditioning. Your Paris experience will be more memorable with a welcoming oasis to call home.

RUE CLER AREA—A safe, tidy, upscale area near the Eiffel Tower; Métro stops Ecole Militaire, La Tour Maubourg, and Invalides	
$$$ Hôtel Relais Bosquet*** 19 Rue du Champ de Mars tel. 01 47 05 25 45 www.hotel-paris-bosquet.com	Exceptionally good hotel with comfortable public spaces and large rooms, RS%
$$$ Hôtel du Cadran*** 10 Rue du Champ de Mars tel. 01 40 62 67 00 www.cadranhotel.com	Perfectly located, over-the-top modern with stylish rooms, RS%
$$$ Hôtel Cadran colors*** 16 Rue Valadon tel. 01 40 62 67 00 www.cadranhotel.com	Cute and quiet with 12 pleasing rooms, near Rue Cler, RS%
$$$ Grand Hôtel Lévêque** 29 Rue Cler tel. 01 47 05 49 15 www.hotel-leveque.com	Busy hotel with average rooms right on Rue Cler
$$ Hôtel Beaugency*** 21 Rue Duvivier tel. 01 47 05 01 63 www.hotel-beaugency.com	Good value on quiet street near Rue Cler, small rooms, RS%
$$ Hôtel du Champ de Mars*** 7 Rue du Champ de Mars tel. 01 45 51 52 30 www.hotelduchampdemars.com	Plush little hotel with hands-on owners, snug but lovingly kept rooms, no A/C
$$$$ Hôtel Duquesne Eiffel*** 23 Avenue Duquesne tel. 01 44 42 09 09 www.hde.fr	Hospitable and expertly run with handsome rooms and welcoming lobby, RS%
$$$ Hôtel Eiffel Turenne*** 20 Avenue de Tourville tel. 01 47 05 99 92 www.hotel-turenne-paris.com	Humble but well-situated with good rooms and several true single rooms

$$$$ Hôtel de Londres Eiffel*** 1 Rue Augereau tel. 01 45 51 63 02 www.hotel-paris-londres-eiffel.com	Close to Eiffel Tower with immaculate, warmly decorated rooms and helpful staff
$$ Hôtel de la Tour Eiffel** 17 Rue de l'Exposition tel. 01 47 05 14 75 www.hotel-toureiffel.com	Terrific value, quiet street, comfortable rooms, no breakfast
$$ Hôtel Kensington** 79 Avenue de la Bourdonnais tel. 01 47 05 74 00 www.hotel-kensington.com	Fair budget hotel near Eiffel Tower, classic two-star comfort, no A/C
$$$$ Hôtel Les Jardins d'Eiffel*** 8 Rue Amélie tel. 01 47 05 46 21 www.hoteljardinseiffel.com	Modern hotel with spacious and peaceful rooms on a quiet street, RS%
$$$ Hôtel Muguet*** 11 Rue Chevert tel. 01 47 05 05 93 www.hotelmuguet.com	Peaceful refuge with tasteful rooms and garden courtyard; strict cancellation policy
$$$ Hôtel de l'Empereur** 2 Rue Chevert tel. 01 45 55 88 02 www.hotelempereurparis.com	Smashing views of Invalides from plush rooms; strict cancellation policy
MARAIS AREA—Classy mansions alongside trendy boutiques create a Greenwich Village vibe; Métro stops Bastille, St-Paul, and Hôtel de Ville	
$$$ Hôtel Castex*** 5 Rue Castex tel. 01 42 72 31 52 www.castexhotel.com	Quiet street, comfortable but narrow, tile-floored rooms, family suites
$$$$ Hôtel Bastille Spéria*** 1 Rue de la Bastille tel. 01 42 72 04 01 www.hotelsperia.com	Ideally located business-class hotel with modern, well-configured rooms

$$$ Hôtel de Neuve*** 14 Rue de Neuve tel. 01 44 59 28 50 www.hoteldeneuveparis.com	Dignified place with classical music in lobby, plush rooms, high tea in afternoon
$$$$ Hôtel Jeanne d'Arc*** 3 Rue de Jarente tel. 01 48 87 62 11 www.hoteljeannedarc.com	Lovely little hotel with thoughtfully appointed rooms, great location, no A/C
$$ Hôtel Daval** 21 Rue Daval tel. 01 47 00 51 23 www.hoteldaval.com	Small rooms, narrow halls, and good rates; streetside rooms can be loud
¢ MIJE Fourcy 6 Rue de Fourcy tel. 01 42 74 23 45 www.mije.com	Hostel, all ages with at least one 18-year-old or older, well-located, clean dorm rooms, prices per person
¢ MIJE Maubisson 12 Rue des Barres tel. 01 42 74 23 45 www.mije.com	Small, quiet hostel with same rates as MIJE Fourcy
$$$ Hôtel de la Bretonnerie*** 22 Rue Ste. Croix de la Bretonnerie tel. 01 48 87 77 63 www.hotelparismaraisbretonnerie.com	Welcoming lobby, good-value rooms with character, no A/C
$$ Hôtel Beaubourg*** 11 Rue Simon Le Franc tel. 01 42 74 34 24 www.hotelbeaubourg.com	Terrific value on a quiet street in the shadow of the Pompidou Center
$$ Hôtel de Nice** 42 bis Rue de Rivoli tel. 01 42 78 55 29 www.hoteldenice.com	On busy main drag; colorful decor, thoughtful touches, and tight bathrooms
$$ Hôtel du Loiret*** 8 Rue des Mauvais Garçons tel. 01 48 87 77 00 www.hotel-du-loiret.fr	Rare Marais budget hotel, noisy but sharp rooms, no A/C

ILE ST. LOUIS AREA—Island in the Seine near Notre-Dame: peaceful, residential, and pricey; Métro stops Pont Marie and Sully-Morland

$$$$ Hôtel du Jeu de Paume** 54 Rue St. Louis-en-l'Ile tel. 01 43 26 14 18 www.jeudepaumehotel.com	Wonderful location, magnificent place with half-timbered lobby and tasteful rooms
$$$$ Hôtel de Lutèce* 65 Rue St. Louis-en-l'Ile tel. 01 43 26 23 52 www.hoteldelutece.com	Cozy lobby with a real fireplace, traditional and warm rooms
$$$$ Hôtel des Deux-Iles* 59 Rue St. Louis-en-l'Ile tel. 01 43 26 13 35 www.hoteldesdeuxiles.com	Bright and colorful, with small but stylish rooms

LUXEMBOURG GARDEN AREA—Left Bank energy with shops, cafés, and the park; Métro stops Cluny-La Sorbonne, St. Sulpice, Mabillon, and Odéon

$$$$ Hôtel le Récamier** 3 bis Place St. Sulpice tel. 01 43 26 04 89 www.hotelrecamier.com	Boutique hotel on Place St. Sulpice, snazzy rooms and public spaces
$$$$ Hôtel de l'Abbaye** 10 Rue Cassette tel. 01 45 44 38 11 www.hotelabbayeparis.com	Lovely refuge with sumptuous rooms and public spaces, includes breakfast
$$$ Hôtel Bonaparte* 61 Rue Bonaparte tel. 01 43 26 97 37 www.hotelbonaparte.fr	Unpretentious, welcoming place with Old World rooms at good prices
$$ Hôtel Jean Bart** 9 Rue Jean-Bart tel. 01 45 48 29 13 www.hotel-jean-bart.fr	Basic hotel near Luxembourg Garden, includes breakfast, no A/C
$$$$ Hôtel Relais Médicis* 5 Place de l'Odéon tel. 01 43 26 00 60 www.relaismedicis.com	Refuge with Old World charm near Odéon Theater, includes breakfast

Sleeping

$$ Hôtel des Grandes Ecoles*** 75 Rue du Cardinal Lemoine tel. 01 43 26 79 23 www.hotel-grandes-ecoles.com	Lovely rooms around a peaceful, flowery courtyard, no A/C
$$ Hôtel des 3 Collèges** 16 Rue Cujas tel. 01 43 54 67 30 www.3colleges.fr	Bright lobby, narrow hallways, and plain rooms at fair rates
$$ Hôtel Cujas Panthéon** 18 Rue Cujas tel. 01 43 54 58 10 www.cujas-pantheon-paris-hotel.com	Traditional comfort at affordable prices
$ Hôtel Cluny Sorbonne** 8 Rue Victor Cousin tel. 01 43 54 66 66 www.hotel-cluny.fr	Modest, warmly run place across from the Sorbonne, thin walls, no A/C
$$$ Hôtel des Mines** 125 Boulevard St. Michel tel. 01 43 54 32 78 www.hoteldesminesparis.com	Less central but a good value, comfortable rooms at fair prices

BOTTOM OF RUE MOUFFETARD—Blue-collar by day, bohemian at night; not so central, but a good value; Métro stops Censier-Daubenton and Les Gobelins

$ Port-Royal-Hôtel* 8 Boulevard de Port-Royal tel. 01 43 31 70 06 www.hotelportroyal.fr	Immaculate hotel on busy street with comfortable rooms, cash only, no A/C
$ Hôtel de L'Espérance** 15 Rue Pascal tel. 01 47 07 10 99 www.hoteldelesperance.fr	Terrific value with quiet, cushy rooms, and pleasing public spaces
¢ Young & Happy Hostel 80 Rue Mouffetard tel. 01 47 07 47 07 www.youngandhappy.fr	Easygoing hostel with kitchen facilities, basic conditions, no A/C, rates per person

MONTMARTRE AREA—Lively, untouristy base of the hill, great for young and budget travelers; Métro stops Abbesses, Anvers, Blanche, and Pigalle	
$$ Hôtel Regyn's Montmartre**** 18 Place des Abbesses tel. 01 42 54 45 21 www.hotel-regyns-paris.com	Small, comfortable rooms with mediocre bathrooms at good rates, no A/C
$ Hôtel André Gill**** 4 Rue André Gill tel. 01 42 62 48 48 www.hotelandregill.com	Bright rooms, alarmingly dark hallways and elevators, good for families
¢ Plug-Inn Boutique Hostel 7 Rue Aristide Bruant tel. 01 42 58 42 58 www.plug-inn.fr	Hostel-like hotel, includes breakfast, kitchen facilities, rates per person
$ Hôtel Bonséjour Montmartre 11 Rue Burq tel. 01 42 54 22 53 www.hotel-bonsejour-montmartre.fr	Old place with some renovations, shared bathrooms, and dirt-cheap prices, no A/C, no elevator, RS%

Sleeping

Eating

The Parisian eating scene is kept at a rolling boil. Entire books (and lives) are dedicated to the subject, and trendy chefs are stalked by the *paparazzi*. Parisians eat long and well. Relaxed lunches, three-hour dinners, and endless hours of sitting in outdoor cafés are the norm. Budget some money—and time—to sightseeing for your palate. Even if the rest of you is sleeping in a cheap hotel, let your taste buds travel first-class in Paris.

I list a full range of restaurants and eateries, from budget options for a quick bite to multicourse splurges with maximum ambience. My listings are in Paris' atmospheric neighborhoods, handy to recommended hotels and sights.

Restaurant Price Code

$$$$	**Splurge:** Most main courses over €25
$$$	**Pricier:** €20-25
$$	**Moderate:** €15-20
$	**Budget:** Under €15

Based on the average cost of a typical main course. A crêpe stand or other takeout spot is **$**; a sit-down brasserie, café, or bistro with afford-able *plats du jour* is **$$**; a casual but more upscale restaurant is **$$$**; and a swanky splurge is **$$$$**.

When in Paris...

When in Paris, I eat on the Parisian schedule. For breakfast, I eat at the hotel or belly up to a café counter for a quick *café au lait* and croissant. Lunch (12:00-14:00) may be a big salad or *plat du jour,* or an atmospheric picnic. In the late afternoon, Parisians enjoy a beverage at a sidewalk table. Dinner is the time for slowing down and savoring a multicourse restaurant meal.

Restaurants

Restaurants and bistros start serving dinner to tourists around 19:00 (a few at 18:30), to locals after 20:00, and can be packed by 21:00. Many restaurants close Sunday and/or Monday. All café and restaurant interiors are smoke-free, but outdoor tables can be smoky.

A full restaurant meal comes in courses. It might include an *apéri-tif* (before-dinner drink), an *entrée* (appetizer), a *plat* (main dish), cheese course, dessert, coffee, liqueurs, several different wines, and so on.

It's not obligatory to order every course—in fact, many Parisians these days consider two courses (e.g., *plat* and dessert) a "full" meal. Ordering as little as a single main dish as your entire meal is acceptable. Couples could each order a *plat* and share a starter or dessert. If you want to eat lighter than that, try a café or brasserie instead. Since even a two- or three-course restaurant meal can take hours, and the costs can add up quickly, plan your strategy before sitting down to a full meal.

Most restaurants offer a good-value *"menu" or "formule"*—a

multicourse meal at a fixed price where you can choose from a list of select items. In addition, many places serve a daily special *plat du jour* (a main dish plus a side, on a single plate), though it may only be offered at lunch.

Parisians are willing to pay for bottled water with their meal *(eau minérale),* but a free carafe of tap water *(une carafe d'eau)* is always available upon request, and more bread is also free.

The service charge is automatically built into your bill's total, so there's no need to tip. For exceptional service, you could tip up to 5 percent, though Parisians rarely do. Waiters probably won't overwhelm you with friendliness or attention—it's not the French style.

To get the most out of your Parisian restaurant—slow down. Allow ample time for the meal, engage the waiter, show you're serious about food, consider his or her recommendations, and enjoy the experience as much as the food itself. *Bon appétit.*

To get a waiter's attention, try to make meaningful eye contact, raise your hand and say, *"S'il vous plaît"*—"please." This phrase should also work when asking for the check—*"L'addition, s'il vous plaît."* In French eateries, a waiter will rarely bring you the check unless you request it. For a French person, having the bill dropped off before asking for it is akin to being kicked out—*très gauche.*

Cafés and Brasseries

Less formal than restaurants, these places serve user-friendly meals, as well as coffee and drinks. They serve food throughout the day, and you're welcome to order just a single dish (even for dinner), rather than a multicourse meal.

Feel free to order a *plat* (main course), a *plat du jour* (daily special), a salad (they're usually big), a sandwich (e.g. a *croque monsieur,* or grilled ham and cheese sandwich), an omelet, an *entrée* (appetizer), or a bowl of soup. It's also fine to split starters and desserts, though not main courses. Many cafés and brasseries have outdoor tables (with braziers in winter), perfect for nursing a glass of wine or *café au lait,* and watching the parade of passersby. A *crêperie*—serving both sweet dessert crêpes and meal-like savory ones—is another less formal, budget alternative.

Be aware that you'll pay more for drinks if you consume them while sitting at a table *(salle)* instead of standing at the bar *(comptoir).* Outdoor tables can sometimes be more expensive still. The prices will

always be clearly posted. Don't sit without first checking out the financial consequences.

Picnicking

Paris makes it easy to turn a picnic into a first-class affair. Takeout delis (a *charcuterie* or *traiteur,* as well as some bakeries) sell high-quality cooked dishes, quiches, pâtés, small pizzas, and salads you can build a meal around. The deli can warm it up for you (*chauffé* = heated up) and pack it in a takeout box *(une barquette),* along with a plastic fork *(fourchette).*

For side dishes, a generic *supermarché* is easy for one-stop shopping, but you'll do better browsing a *boulangerie* for your baguette, a *fromagerie* for cheese, and an open-air market for the freshest produce.

Be daring. Try the smelly cheeses, ugly pâtés, and sissy quiches. Some good picnic spots in the heart of Paris are the Palais Royal courtyard, the Place des Vosges, the west tip of Ile de la Cité, and the Tuileries Garden.

French Cuisine

You can be a galloping gourmet and try several types of French cuisine without ever leaving the confines of Paris. Most restaurants serve dishes from several regions, though some focus on a particular region's cuisine.

From Burgundy (among France's best cuisines), try *coq au vin* (rooster with red wine sauce), *bœuf bourguignon* (beef stew), or *escargots.* From Normandy and Brittany you'll find mussels and oysters, crêpes, and cider. Any dish prepared *à la provençale* features that region's garlic, olive oil, herbs, and tomatoes. You'll find *bouillabaisse* from the Côte d'Azur, *pâté de foie gras* (goose-liver pâté) from the southwest, and even Alsatian *choucroute*—sauerkraut.

Paris has a particular fondness for steak, including steak tartare—raw ground beef. Duck from the Dordogne region *(confit de canard)*, leg of lamb *(gigot d'agneau)*, roasted chicken *(poulet roti)*, and salmon *(saumon)* are also popular. Raw oysters *(huîtres)* from Brittany are a Christmas tradition. Sauces are a huge part of French cooking. The five classics are *béchamel* (milk-based white sauce), *espagnole* (veal-based brown sauce), *velouté* (stock-based white sauce), *tomate* (tomato-based red sauce), and *hollandaise* (egg yolk-based white sauce).

Commonly served cheeses are Brie de Meaux (mild and creamy, from just outside Paris), Camembert (semicreamy and pungent, from Normandy), *chèvre* (goat cheese with a sharp taste, from the Loire), and Roquefort (strong and blue-veined, from south-central France). Many restaurants will bring you a variety platter you can choose from.

For dessert, try a *café gourmand*, an assortment of small desserts selected by the restaurant. Other classic desserts include *crème bruleé, tarte tatin,* and *mousse au chocolat.*

No meal in France is complete without wine. Even the basic table wine *(vin du pays)* is fine with a meal—order it by the pitcher, or *pichet*. For good-but-inexpensive wines by the bottle, look for reds from Côtes du Rhone or Languedoc, and whites from Burgundy or Alsace. In summer, everyone should try an inexpensive rosé. Those willing to pay more can get a good (but not cheap) pinot noir from Burgundy, or a heavier red from Bordeaux.

The French do not drink wine as *apéritifs.* More common are champagne, beer, a Kir (a dash of crème de Cassis with white wine), or Pastis (an anise-flavored liquor from Provence). France's best beer is Alsatian; try Kronenbourg or the heavier Pelfort. *Une panaché* is a refreshing French shandy (lemon soda and beer).

For coffee, Parisians like *un café* (shot of espresso), a *café au lait/café crème* (espresso with lots of steamed milk), or *une noisette* (espresso with a shot of milk). A fun, bright, nonalcoholic drink is *un diablo menthe,* featuring 7-Up with mint syrup. If you're ordering a Coke, remember that Paris' last ice cubes melted after the last Yankee tour group left.

RUE CLER AREA—Eateries catering to upscale residents near the Eiffel Tower (see map, page 192)

➊	**$ Café du Marché** 38 Rue Cler tel. 01 47 05 51 27	High-energy, great outdoor seating right on Rue Cler (Mon-Sat 11:00-23:00, Sun 11:00-17:00)
➋	**$$ Tribeca Restaurant** Located next to Café du Marché tel. 01 45 55 12 01	Same owners as Café du Marché, with Italian theme (open daily)
➌	**$ Le Petit Cler** 29 Rue Cler tel. 01 45 50 17 50	Tiny, traditional café with leather booths, fine food, and a few outdoor tables (open daily)
➍	**$ Crêperie Ulysée en Gaule** 28 Rue Cler tel. 01 47 05 61 82	Cheapest seats on Rue Cler with crêpes to go (open daily)
➎	**$$$ Le Florimond** 19 Avenue de la Motte-Picquet tel. 01 45 55 40 38	Intimate and welcoming, with classic French cuisine, reservations smart (closed Sun and first and third Sat of month)
➏	**$$$ Au Petit Tonneau** 20 Rue Surcouf tel. 01 47 05 09 01	Small bistro with real-deal ambience, limited but good selections (closed Mon)
➐	**$$ Café le Bosquet** 46 Avenue Bosquet tel. 01 45 51 38 13	Modern brasserie with dressy waiters, sit inside or out, good-value menu (closed Sun)
➑	**$$$ La Terrasse du 7ème** 2 Place de L'Ecole Militaire tel. 01 45 55 00 02	Busy café with grand outdoor seating and a living-room interior (open daily until at least 24:00)
➒	**$$$ Bistrot Belhara** 23 Rue Duvivier tel. 01 45 51 41 77 www.bistrotbelhara.com	Vintage French dining experience with inventive and classic dishes in an intimate setting (closed Sun-Mon)
➓	**$$$ Au Petit Sud Ouest** 46 Avenue de la Bourdonnais tel. 01 45 55 59 59	Wood-beam coziness for southwestern specialties: foie gras, cassoulet, duck (closed Sun-Mon)
⓫	**$$$$ 58 Tour Eiffel** Mo: Bir-Hakeim or Trocadéro tel. 01 72 76 18 46	Snazzy place in the Eiffel Tower (first floor), reserve way ahead for view tables (open daily)

⑫	**$$$ Le P'tit Troquet** 28 Rue de l'Exposition tel. 01 47 05 80 39	Charming, intimate, and welcoming bistro with 1920s elegance and wonderful meals (opens at 18:30, closed Sun)
⑬	**$$ Café Constant** 139 Rue St. Dominique tel. 01 47 53 73 34	Cool, two-level place with delicious and affordable dishes (open daily)
⑭	**$$$$ Le Violon d'Ingres** 135 Rue St. Dominique tel. 01 45 55 15 05	Chef Christian Constant serves top cuisine in a modern setting, reservations essential (open daily)
⑮	**$$ Café de Mars** 11 Rue Augereau tel. 01 45 50 10 90 www.cafedemars.com	Reasonably priced meals in relaxed atmosphere, comfortable for single diners (closed Sun)
MARAIS AREA—Trendy places amid boisterous nightlife (see map, page 194)		
⑯	**$$$ Vin des Pyrénées** 25 Rue Beautreillis tel. 01 42 72 64 94	Authentic dishes presented in a lighthearted, Rembrandt-like setting (open daily)
⑰	**$$ Café Hugo** 22 Place des Vosges tel. 01 42 72 64 04	Basic café fare in a terrific setting, fun energy (open daily)
⑱	**$$$ La Place Royale** 2 bis Place des Vosges tel. 01 42 78 58 16	On the square, warm welcome, good-value wines and menus (open daily)
⑲	**$$$ Le Petit Marché** 9 Rue du Béarn tel. 01 42 72 06 67	Cozy and intimate bistro with friendly service, serving French classics with an Asian influence (open daily)
⑳	**$$$ Brasserie Bofinger** 5 Rue de la Bastille tel. 01 42 72 87 82 www.bofingerparis.com	Vintage, sprawling place famous for fish and traditional cuisine with Alsatian flair (open daily)
㉑	**$$$ Chez Janou** 2 Rue Roger Verlomme tel. 01 42 72 28 41	Lively Provençal bistro with Mediterranean cuisine, sit inside or out (open daily)

㉒	**$$ Les Bougresses** 6 Rue de Jarente tel. 01 48 87 71 21	Fun-loving place with good-value food, just off Place du Marché Ste. Catherine (open daily from 18:30)
㉓	**$$$ Le Temps des Cerises** 31 Rue de la Cerisaie tel. 01 42 72 08 63	Local wine bar with 1950s character, tight seating, and tasty food (open daily)
㉔	**$ La Droguerie** 56 Rue des Rosiers	Hole-in-the-wall crêpe stand, dine in or take away (daily 12:00-22:00)
㉕	**$$ Le Marché** and **Au Bistrot de la Place** Place du Marché Ste. Catherine	Two fun, cheap places on the Marais' most romantic and charming square (both open daily)
㉖	**$$ Breizh Café** 109 Rue du Vieille du Temple tel. 01 42 72 13 77	Simple Breton place with delicious organic crêpes, sparkling cider (11:30 to late, closed Mon-Tue)
㉗	**$$ Chez Marianne** 2 Rue des Hospitalières-St.-Gervais tel. 01 42 72 18 86	Blends delicious Jewish cuisine with Parisian élan in a cluttered wine shop (open long hours daily)
㉘	**$ Le Loir dans la Théière** 3 Rue des Rosiers tel. 01 42 72 90 61	Cozy teahouse for baked goods, hot drinks, and weekend brunch (daily 9:00-19:00)
㉙	**$ L'As du Fallafel** 34 Rue des Rosiers tel. 01 48 87 63 60	Best falafel in the Jewish Quarter, as well as other tasty dishes (long hours, closed Fri eve and Sat)
㉚	**$$$$ Au Bourguignon du Marais** 52 Rue Francois Miron tel. 01 48 87 15 40	Dressy wine-bar/bistro with fine cuisine, ideal for Burgundy-lovers (open daily)
㉛	**$$ L'Ebouillanté** 6 Rue des Barres tel. 01 42 74 70 57	Breezy, romantic crêperie-café (open daily 12:00-21:30)
ILE ST. LOUIS—Quiet, romantic area perfect for after-dinner strolling (see map, page 194)		
㉜	**$$$ Les Fous de l'Ile** 33 Rue des Deux Ponts tel. 01 43 25 76 67	Fun place for bistro fare with gourmet touches at a good price (open daily)

㉝	**$$ Nos Ancêtres les Gaulois** 39 Rue St. Louis-en-l'Ile tel. 01 46 33 66 07	All you can eat and drink for €40 in a rowdy, medieval cellar (open daily)
㉞	**$$ La Brasserie de l'Ile St. Louis** 55 Quai de Bourbon tel. 01 43 54 02 59	Purely Alsatian cuisine served in a vigorous, hunting-lodge setting (closed Wed)
㉟	**$$$ L'Orangerie** 28 Rue St. Louis-en-l'Ile tel. 01 46 33 93 98	Inviting place with soft lighting, comfortable seating, and traditional cuisine (closed Mon)
㊱	**$$ Auberge de la Reine Blanche** 30 Rue St. Louis-en-l'Ile tel. 01 46 33 07 87	Tasty cuisine at reasonable prices in a cozy setting (closed Wed)
㊲	**$ Café Med** 77 Rue St. Louis-en-l'Ile tel. 01 43 29 73 17	Inexpensive salads, crêpes, and plats in a tight but cheery setting (open daily)
LUXEMBOURG GARDEN AREA—Lively near St. Sulpice, quieter near Panthéon (see map, page 194)		
㊳	**$ Pasta Luna** 15 Rue Mézières tel. 01 45 44 32 02	Yummy deli specializing in Corsican fare, sandwiches to order (open 11:00 until the bread runs out around 19:00, closed Sun)
㊴	**$$ Chez Fernand** 13 Rue Guisarde	Friendly French bistro fare
㊵	**$$ Boucherie Roulière** 24 Rue des Canettes	Affordable steaks in a fun neighborhood setting
㊶	**$$$ Les Deux Magots** and **Le Café de Flore** Place St. Germain-des-Prés	Two famous cafés on a famous boulevard with a famous clientele (open daily)
㊷	**$$$ La Méditerranée** 2 Place de l'Odéon tel. 01 43 26 02 30	Gourmet seafood in lovely and dressy setting, Odéon view, reservations smart (open daily)
㊸	**$ Restaurant Polidor** 41 Rue Monsieur-le-Prince tel. 01 43 26 95 34	Bare-bones bistro with unpretentious cooking and fun old-Paris atmosphere (open daily)

Rue Cler Area Restaurants

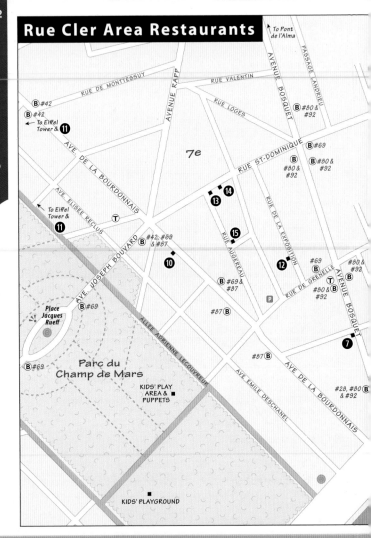

To Pont
de l'Alma

Eating

RUE DE MONTTESSUY

RUE VALENTIN

AVENUE RAPP

AVENUE BOSQUET

PASSAGE LANDRIEU

Ⓑ #42

Ⓑ #42

← To Eiffel
Tower & ⑪

RUE LOGES

Ⓑ #80 &
#92

AVE. DE LA BOURDONNAIS

7e

RUE ST-DOMINIQUE

Ⓑ #69

Ⓑ #80 &
#92

AVE. ELISEE RECLUS

Ⓣ

To Eiffel
Tower & ⑪

Ⓑ #42, #69
& #87

AVE. JOSEPH BOUVARD

⑬ ⑭

⑮

RUE AIGEREAU

RUE DE LA EXPOSITION

⑩

Ⓑ #69 &
#87

⑫

#69

Ⓑ #80 &
#92

Ⓣ
Ⓑ #80 &
#92

AVENUE BOSQUET

Ⓑ #69

Place
Jacques
Rueff

RUE DE GRENELLE

Ⓟ

#87 Ⓑ

Ⓑ #69

Parc du
Champ de Mars

ALLEE ADRIENNE LECOUVREUR

#87 Ⓑ

AVE. DE LA BOURDONNAIS

❼

AVE. EMILE DESCHANEL

#28, #80
& #92 Ⓑ

KIDS' PLAY
AREA &
PUPPETS

KIDS' PLAYGROUND

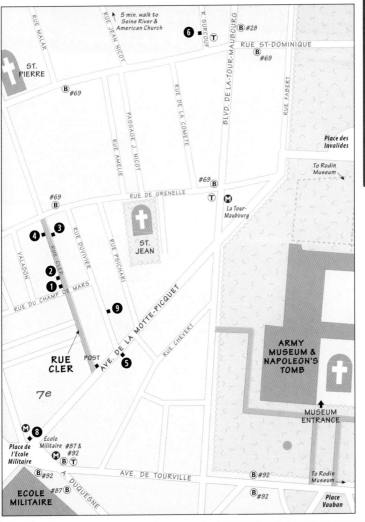

Marais, Ile St. Louis &
Luxembourg Garden Restaurants

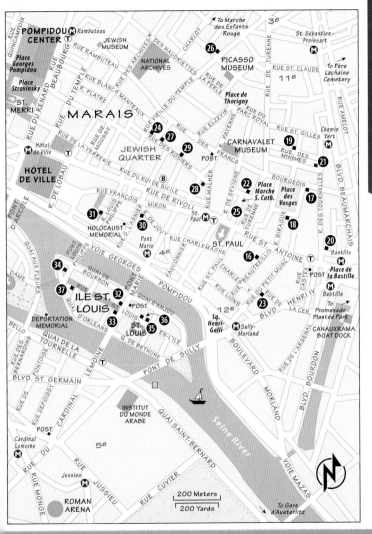

Practicalities

PLANNING

Paris' best travel months—also the busiest and most expensive for flights and hotels—are May, June, September, and October. The summer heat in July and August can be unpleasant (though hotel rates can drop). Paris makes a great winter getaway. Although it's cold and rainy, crowds are less, cafés are cozy, and the city feels lively but not touristy.

Make sure your passport is up to date (to renew, see www.travel.state.gov). Call your debit- and credit-card companies about your plans. Book hotel rooms well in advance, especially for peak season (May, June, Sept, Oct) and holidays. Consider buying travel insurance. Book an entrance time at the Eiffel Tower to avoid long lines. If you're traveling beyond Paris, research rail passes, TGV train reservations, and car rentals.

MONEY

France uses the euro currency: 1 euro (€1) = about $1.20. To convert euros to dollars add about 20 percent: €20 = about $24, €50 = about $60. (Check www.oanda.com for the latest exchange rates.)

Withdraw money from an ATM (known as a *distributeur* in France) using a debit card, just like at home. Visa and MasterCard are commonly used throughout Europe. Before departing, call your bank or credit-card company: Ask about international transaction fees, alert them that you'll be making withdrawals in Europe, and get your credit card's PIN. Many travelers bring a second debit or credit card as a backup.

While American credit cards are accepted almost everywhere in Europe, even newer chip-style cards may not work in some payment machines (e.g., ticket kiosks). Be prepared to pay with cash, find a nearby cashier, or try entering your credit card's PIN.

To keep your valuables safe, wear a money belt. But if you do lose your credit or debit card, report the loss immediately with a phone call to these toll-free numbers in France: Visa (tel. 08 00 90 11 79), MasterCard (tel. 08 00 90 13 87), and American Express (tel. 01 47 77 70 00).

Practicalities

Helpful Websites

Paris' Tourist Information: www.parisinfo.com
France's Tourist Information: http://us.france.fr
Passports and Red Tape: www.travel.state.gov
Cheap Flights: www.kayak.com (for international flights),
www.skyscanner.com (for flights within Europe)
Airplane Carry-on Restrictions: www.tsa.gov
European Train Schedules: www.bahn.com
General Travel Tips: www.ricksteves.com (helpful info on train travel,
railpasses, car rental, travel insurance, packing lists, and much more—
plus updates to this book)

ARRIVAL IN PARIS

Charles de Gaulle Airport

Paris' main airport has three terminals: T-1, T-2, and T-3. All have ATMs, banks, shops, and bars. There are Paris Tourisme offices in T-1 (arrivals hall, door 6) and T-2, as well as helpful ADP info desks. You can travel between terminals for free on the CDGVAL shuttle train or by shuttle bus (allow 30 minutes to travel between terminals and hour total travel time between gates at T-1 and T-2). For airport information, visit www.adp.fr (airport code: CDG).

To get between any of the airport's three terminals and downtown Paris, you have several options:

Taxi/Uber: Taxis charge a flat rate into Paris (€55 to the Left Bank, €50 to the Right Bank for up to four people with bags; supplement for extra passengers). For trips from Paris to the airport, have your hotel arrange it a day in advance. Paris Uber offers airport pickup or drop-off, but can't use the bus-only lanes as taxis can, so expect some added time (€30-80).

Roissy-Bus: Buses make the 50-minute trip to the Opéra Métro stop in central Paris, arriving on Rue Scribe (€11, 3-4/hour, runs 6:00-23:00, buy ticket at airport Paris Tourisme desk, ticket machine, or on bus). From there, it's an easy Métro ride to anywhere in the city.

Le Bus Direct: Bus #2 goes to Etoile/Arc de Triomphe and Porte Maillot (50 minutes). Bus #4 runs to Gare de Lyon (45 minutes) and the Montparnasse

Tower/train station (1.25 hours) All stops are on Métro lines (€17 one-way, 2/ hour, runs 5:45-22:30, toll tel. 08 92 35 08 20, www.lebusdirect.com).

RER-B Trains: This option is cheaper but more complicated. Follow *Paris by Train* signs, then *RER* signs. The train serves Gare du Nord, Châtelet-Les Halles, St. Michel, and Luxembourg (€11, 4/hour, runs 5:00-24:00, about 35 minutes).

Airport Vans: Shuttle vans carry passengers to or from their hotels, with stops along the way to pick up other passengers. They cost about €32 for one person, €46 for two, or €58 for three. Ask your hotel to arrange one at last a day in advance. Several companies offer shuttle service; I usually just go with the one my hotel uses.

Other Arrival Points

Orly Airport: Paris' second airport is smaller, but its two terminals—Ouest (west) and Sud (south)—have all the conveniences. Helpful orange ADP information desks are near baggage claim. For flight info visit www.adp.fr (airport code: ORY). To get into Paris, you can take a taxi (€30 to Left Bank, €35 to Right Bank); or catch the Le Bus Direct to Gare Montparnasse, La Motte-Picquet (near Rue Cler), Eiffel Tower, Trocadéro, or Arc de Triomphe/ Etoile (€12, buy ticket from driver or book online, 4/hour, 40 minutes).

Paris' Train Stations: Paris has six major stations, each serving different regions. For example, to go to London on the Eurostar, you leave from Gare du Nord. Trains to Chartres leave from Gare Montparnasse. The best all-Europe train schedule information is online at www.bahn.com. The French national rail website is www.sncf.com. Book TGV trains well in advance at www.tgv-europe.com. To see if a railpass could save you money, check www.ricksteves.com/rail.

HELPFUL HINTS

Tourist Information (TI): Don't go out of your way tracking down Paris' official TIs, which often have long lines. But if you do come across one (e.g., at Charles de Gaulle airport), pick up a free map and consider buying a Museum Pass (www.parisinfo.com).

Bookstores: English-language bookstores include the venerable **Shakespeare and Company** (near Notre-Dame, 37 Rue de la Bûcherie, tel. 01 43 25 40 93); **W. H. Smith** alongside the Tuileries Garden (248 Rue

Tipping

Tipping in France isn't as generous as it is in the US. To tip a taxi driver, round up to the next euro on the fare (for a €13 fare, give €14). For longer rides, figure about 10 percent.

For sit-down service in a restaurant, a 12-15 percent service charge is always already included in the list price of the food (*service compris*). Most Parisians never tip. However, if you feel the service was *exceptional,* it's fine to tip up to 5 percent extra. When you hand your payment plus a tip to your waiter, you can say, *"C'est bon"* (say bohn), meaning, "It's good." If you are using a credit card, leave your tip in cash—credit-card receipts don't even have a space to add a tip.

In general, if someone in the tourism or service industry does a super job for you, a small tip of a euro or two is appropriate...but not required.

de Rivoli, Mo: Concorde, tel. 01 44 77 88 99); and the **San Francisco Book Company** near Luxembourg Garden (17 Rue Monsieur le Prince, Mo: Odéon, tel. 01 43 29 15 70).

Hurdling the Language Barrier: Most Parisians speak some English—certainly more English than Americans speak French. Still, learn the pleasantries like *bonjour* (good day), *pardon* (pardon me), *s'il vous plaît* (please), *merci* (thank you), and *au revoir* (goodbye). Begin every encounter with *"Bonjour, Madame* or *Monsieur,"* or *"s'il vous plaît,"* and ask *"Parlez-vous anglais?"* End every encounter with *"Au revoir, Madame* or *Monsieur."* For more French survival phrases, ✪ see page 217.

Time: France's time zone is six/nine hours ahead of the East/West Coasts of the US.

Business Hours: Most businesses are open Monday through Saturday, roughly 10:00-19:00. Smaller shops may close for lunch (12:00-14:00). Banks close on Sunday and possibly Monday. On Sunday morning, some small markets, *boulangeries* (bakeries), and street markets are open until noon. Handy hole-in-the-wall grocery stores stay open every day until midnight.

Watt's Up? Europe's electrical system is 220 volts, instead of North America's 110 volts. You'll need an adapter plug with two round prongs, sold inexpensively at travel stores in the US. Most newer electronics convert automatically, so you won't need a separate converter.

Laundry: Paris has no shortage of self-serve launderettes—ask your hotelier for the closest one.

Pedestrian Safety: Parisian drivers are notorious for ignoring pedestrians. Look both ways. Don't assume you have the right of way, even in a crosswalk. Be aware that many streets are one-way, and be careful of seemingly quiet bus/taxi lanes. Bicycles are silent but dangerous, lurking in the bus/taxi lane or going the wrong way on a one-way street.

WCs: Paris has some free public toilets (tipping the attendant is appropriate) and some coin-op "toilet-booths" along the sidewalks. Otherwise, use restrooms in museums, or walk into any sidewalk café like you own the place, and find the toilet in the back.

Tabacs: These handy little neighborhood shops sell postage stamps, Métro tickets, sometimes Museum Passes, and...oh yeah, cigarettes. They're a slice of workaday Paris.

GETTING AROUND PARIS

In Paris, you're never more than a 10-minute walk from a Métro station, and buses are everywhere. Study the fold-out Métro map at the back of this book, buy a *carnet* of 10 tickets, learn a few handy bus lines, and Paris is yours. For more information on Paris' public transportation system, visit www.ratp.fr.

Buying Tickets

The same ticket works on the Métro, RER suburban trains (within the city), and city buses. A single ticket costs €1.80 and is valid for as many transfers as you need to make a single journey within 90 minutes, provided you don't exit the station (not valid to transfer between Métro/RER and bus).

To save money, buy a *carnet* of 10 tickets for €14.10. Or you could consider the one-day Mobilis pass (€7) or the weekly Passe Navigo, a chip-embedded card (€21.25 plus €5 first-time fee and €5 for ID photo). Which is best? It's hard to beat the *carnet*. Two 10-packs of *carnets*—enough for most travelers staying a week—cost about €28.20 and can be shared between travel partners. The Passe Navigo only becomes worthwhile for visitors who stay a full week (and start their trip early in the week—the pass expires on Sundays) and use the pass for regional trips (it gets you to Versailles and the airport).

Buy tickets and passes at most Métro stations or at some *tabac* shops. Be aware that not every Métro station has a staffed ticket window (where you can buy tickets using cash or American-style magnetic-stripe credit cards). However, all stations have ticket-vending machines that accept coins (and chip-and-PIN credit cards, which few Americans have).

By Métro
Europe's best underground train system runs daily 5:30-1:00 in the morning, Fri-Sat until 2:00 in the morning. Begin by studying a Métro map.

Find the Métro stop closest to you and the stop closest to your destination. Next see which lines connect those two points. The lines are color-coded and numbered, and are known by their end-of-the-line stops.

In the Métro station, signs direct you to the train line going in your direction (e.g., *direction: La Défense*). Insert your ticket in the turnstile, reclaim it, pass through, and hang onto your ticket until you exit the system. To make transfers, follow *correspondance* (connection) signs. Be prepared to walk significant distances within Métro stations. Once you reach your final stop, look for the blue-and-white *sortie* (exit) signs. Use the helpful neighborhood maps to choose the *sortie* closest to where you want to go. After you exit the system, toss or tear your used ticket so you don't confuse it with unused tickets.

Be wary of thieves in the Métro—while you're preoccupied buying tickets, passing through turnstiles, and contending with the jostle of boarding and leaving crowded trains.

By RER: The RER suburban train line works just like the Métro and uses the same ticket (valid within the city center only; transfers OK between Métro and RER). On your Métro map, the RER routes are the thick lines labeled A, B, C, and so on. Many trains don't stop at every station—check the sign over the platform to see if your destination is listed as a stop.

By City Bus
Paris' excellent bus system works like buses anywhere. Every bus stop has a name, and every bus is headed to one end-of-the-line stop or the other. One Zone 1 ticket gets you anywhere in central Paris within the freeway ring road. It's good for transfers between buses within 90 minutes, but not from bus to Métro/RER, or for multiple trips on the same bus line.

Board your bus through the front door. Validate your ticket or scan your Passe Navigo. Push the red button to signal the driver you want a stop, then exit through the central or rear door. Avoid rush hour—Monday-Friday 8:00-9:30 & 17:30-19:30—when the Métro is a better option.

Bus #69 runs east-west between the Eiffel Tower and Père Lachaise Cemetery by way of Rue Cler, the Orsay Museum, the Louvre, and the Marais. Scenic bus #73 runs from the Orsay up the Champs-Elysées to the Arc de Triomphe. I always check the bus stop near my hotel to see if it's convenient to my plans.

By Uber

Uber works in Paris like it does at home, and in general works better than taxis in Paris (www.uber.com). Drivers are nicer and more flexible than taxi drivers, and it's a bit cheaper than a taxi (be warned that peak hour rates are higher). Uber drivers can pick you up anywhere so you don't have to track down a taxi stand, and you can text them if you don't see the car. There's no language problem giving directions, as you can type your destination into the app. Your US app and US Uber accounts will work in Paris as long as you have access to cellular data. The only down-side is that Uber drivers can't use the taxi/bus lanes during rush hour, so your trip may take longer at busy times than it would in a cab.

By Taxi

Parisian taxis are reasonable, especially for couples and families,. Fares and supplements (described in English on the rear windows) are straight-forward and regulated. A taxi can fit four people, or more if you book in advance.

The meter starts at €2.60, and there's a minimum total of €7. A typical 20-minute ride (e.g., Place Bastille to Eiffel Tower) costs about €25. Taxis charge higher rates at rush hour, at night, all day Sunday, and for extra passengers. To tip, round up to the next euro (at least €0.50).

You can try waving down a taxi, or find the nearest taxi stand—they're marked with a   on this book's maps. To order a taxi, call 01 41 27 66 99 (or ask your hotelier); a set fee of €4 is applied for an immediate booking or €7 for reserving in advance. Taxis are tough to find during rush hour, when it's raining, and on weekend nights. If you need to catch an early morning train or flight, book your taxi at least the day before; your hotel can help.

By Bike

Paris is great by bicycle. The city is flat, there are more than 370 miles of bike and bus-priority lanes, and Parisian drivers are growing accustomed to sharing the road.

Rental bikes are everywhere, thanks to the city-wide **Vélib'** program. Anyone can just swipe a debit or credit card (chip-and-PIN or American Express) at one of 1,500 stations, take a bike off the rack, and return it at any station when they're done. Use Vélib' bikes only for short-term rental (a few hours or less), as pricing is structured to discourage longer use. If you want a bike for longer, rent from one of the companies I list next.

You can rent bikes from **Bike About Tours** near Hôtel de Ville (€15/day, 17 Rue du Pont Louis Philippe, www.bikeabouttours.com) or from **Fat Tire Bike Tours** near the Eiffel Tower (€4/hour, 24 Rue Edgar Faure, www.fat-tiretours.com/paris, call 01 82 88 80 96 to check availability). Both outfits also offer good bike tours.

Sunday cycling is especially peaceful: The city opens up many districts just for bikes (see www.paris.fr/parisrespire for details).

STAYING CONNECTED

Bring your own mobile device (phone, tablet, laptop) and follow my budget tips. For more information than what I've provided here, see www.ricksteves.com/phoning.

Making Calls

To call France from the US or Canada: Dial 011 (our international access code) + 33 (France's country code) + the local number, without the initial zero.

To call France from a European country: Dial 00 (Europe's international access code) + 33 followed by the local number, without the initial zero.

To call within France: Just dial the local number (including the initial zero).

To call from France to another country: Dial 00, the country code (for example, 1 for the US or Canada), then the area code and number. If you're calling European countries whose phone numbers begin with 0, you'll usually have to omit that 0 when you dial.

Practicalities

Useful Phone Numbers

Police: Tel. 17
Emergency Medical Assistance: Tel. 15
Directory Assistance (some English spoken): Tel. 12
US Consulate and Embassy: Tel. 01 43 12 22 22, emergency services Mon-Fri 9:00-11:00, 4 Avenue Gabriel, Mo: Concorde, http://france.usembassy.gov
Canadian Consulate and Embassy: Tel. 01 44 43 29 02, 35 Avenue Montaigne, Mo: Franklin D. Roosevelt, www.amb-canada.fr
Collect Calls to the US: Tel. 00 00 11

If you're calling from Europe using your US mobile phone, you can enter a + instead of 00 or 001 (press and hold the 0 key).

Budget Tips for Using a Mobile Device in Europe

Use free Wi-Fi whenever possible. Unless you have an unlimited data plan, save most of your online tasks for Wi-Fi. Many hotels and cafés have Wi-Fi for guests.

Sign up for an international plan. Most providers offer a global plan that cuts the cost of calls and texts, and gives you a block of data. Your normal plan may already include this coverage (T-Mobile's does).

Minimize the use of your cellular network. If you can't find Wi-Fi, you can roam on your cellular network. When you're done, avoid further charges by disabling "data roaming" or "cellular data" in your settings. Save bandwidth-gobbling tasks (Skyping, downloading apps, streaming) for when you're on Wi-Fi.

Use calling/messaging apps for cheaper calls and texts. Some apps (Skype, Viber, FaceTime, Google+ Hangouts) let you call or text for free or cheap.

Use a European SIM card. This option helps you get faster data connections and make voice calls at cheap local rates. Either buy a basic phone in Europe (about $40 from mobile-phone shops) or bring an "unlocked" US phone. In Europe, buy a SIM card to insert in your phone, giving you a European phone number. Buy a new card when you arrive in a new country (sold at phone shops, newsstands, vending machines, and department-store electronics counters).

Finding Wi-Fi in Paris

Most hotels offer some form of free or cheap Internet access—either a shared computer in the lobby or Wi-Fi in the room. You'll also find plenty of Wi-Fi hotspots at cafés and a few museums. In a Parisian café, Wi-Fi works just like at home—you order something, then ask the waiter for the Wi-Fi ("wee-fee") password (*mot de passe;* moh duh pahs). Most public parks offer free Wi-Fi (look for purple *Zone Wi-Fi* signs) with an easy one-time registration (start by selecting the Wi-Fi network, usually called "Paris_WIFI" plus a number). The Orange network also has many hotspots; if you come across one, click "Select Your Pass" to register.

SIGHTSEEING TIPS

Hours: Hours of sights can change unexpectedly; confirm the latest times from a TI, or at the sight's website, or the general website www.parisinfo. com. Many sights stop admitting people 30-60 minutes before closing time, and guards start shooing people out before the actual closing time, so don't save the best for last.

What to Expect: Important sights such as the Louvre have metal detectors or conduct bag searches that will slow your entry. Others require you to check (for free) daypacks and coats. Photos and videos are normally allowed, but flashes or tripods usually are not. Many sights offer guided tours and rent audioguides. Most have an on-site café. Expect changes—artwork can be in restoration, displayed elsewhere, or on tour.

Discounts: Many sights offer free or reduced admission for youths up to age 18 and students (with proper ID cards, www.isic.org). Senior discounts are generally only for EU residents, but it's worth asking— *"Réduction troisième âge?"*

Affording Paris' Sights: Some sights are free (and crowded) on certain Sundays (Louvre, Orsay, Rodin, Cluny, Pompidou Center), while others offer discounts if you enter later in the day (Orsay, Orangerie, Army Museum).

Audioguides and Tours: I've produced free 🎧 audio tours of many of Paris' best sights. With a mobile device, you can take me along as you tour the Louvre, Orsay, Versailles, and historic Paris. You can download Rick Steves Audio Europe via Apple's App Store, Google Play, or the Amazon Appstore.

Paris Museum Pass

In Paris there are two classes of sightseers—those with a Paris Museum Pass, and those who stand in line. The pass admits you to many of Paris' most popular sights, and lets you skip the (often long) ticket-buying lines (but not security lines). You'll save time and money by getting this pass.

A pass covering two consecutive days costs €48; four days is €62; and six days is €74. Buy the pass at participating museums, monuments, TIs, and some souvenir stores. Avoid buying the pass at a major museum (such as the Louvre) with long lines.

Most of Paris' major sights are covered by the pass, including the Louvre, Orsay, Sainte-Chapelle, Picasso Museum, and Versailles. Key sights that are *not* covered are the Eiffel Tower, Montparnasse Tower, Marmottan Museum, Opéra Garnier, and Jacquemart-André Museum. Add up your sightseeing to see if the pass is worth it. The pass can pay for itself with four key admissions in two days. For more info and a full list of covered sights, visit www.parismuseumpass.com.

You can't skip the security lines, though at a few sights (including the Louvre), pass holders may be able to skip to the front. Once past security, look for signs designating the entrance for reserved ticket holders. If it's not obvious, boldly walk to the front of the ticket line, hold up your pass, and ask the ticket-taker: *"Entrez, pass?"* (ahn-tray pahs). You'll either be allowed to enter at that point or directed to a special entrance.

To make the most of your pass, validate it only when you're ready to tackle covered sights on consecutive days. Make sure those sights will be open. Sightsee like mad during your "pass" days by visiting sights open late.

Avoiding Lines with Advance Tickets: Even without a Museum Pass, you can still skip ticket lines at many places with long lines. You can buy individual *"coupe-file"* (line-cutting) tickets at TIs, FNAC department stores, and travel-service companies such as Paris Webservices and Fat Tire Tours. Several sights, such as the Eiffel Tower, Sainte-Chapelle, the Catacombs, and Monet's gardens at Giverny, sell advance tickets online.

THEFT AND EMERGENCIES

Theft: While violent crime is rare in the city center, thieves (mainly pick-pockets) thrive near famous monuments and on the Métro. Be alert to the possibility of theft, even when you're absorbed in the wonder and newness of Paris. Be on guard when crowds press together, especially at tourist sights, while you're preoccupied at ticket windows, and while boarding and leaving buses and subways. Assume any beggar or friendly petitioner is a pickpocket, and that any commotion in a crowd is a distraction to pick-pockets. Smartphones are thief-magnets. I keep my valuables—passport, credit cards, crucial documents, and large amounts of cash—in a money belt that I tuck under my beltline. Muggings are rare, but if you're out late, avoid dimly lit, empty places, such as the dark riverfront embankments.

Dial 17 for English-speaking police help. Claim lost property at the police station (36 Rue des Morillons, Mo: Convention, tel. 08 21 00 25 25). To replace a passport, file a police report, then call your embassy to make an appointment.

Medical Help: In France, dial 15 for an ambulance. For minor ailments, first visit a pharmacy (marked by a green cross), where qualified technicians routinely diagnose and prescribe. For serious problems, ask your hotelier for assistance. Many doctors speak English. The American Hospital is at 63 Boulevard Victor Hugo in the Neuilly suburb (Mo: Porte Maillot, tel. 01 46 41 25 25). SOS Doctors make house calls to hotels or homes (tel. 3624). A list of English-speaking doctors is available on the website of the US Embassy in Paris (http://france.usembassy.gov).

ACTIVITIES

Shopping

Chic Paris has a tradition of marketing some of the world's most elegant, trendy, and overpriced clothes, jewels, and foods. The shops with their window displays are works of art themselves. Stroll some of the fashion-able neighborhoods and indulge in a little window-shopping, which the French call *faire du lèche-vitrines*—"window-licking."

Most shops are open Monday to Saturday 10:00-19:00, although some small shops don't open until 14:00 on Mondays.

Shopping Etiquette: Entering a small shop, greet the clerk with

"*Bonjour, Madame (or Mademoiselle or Monsieur),*" and bid them "*Au revoir*" when leaving. Ask before handling clothing—"*Je peux?*" means "Can I?" It's OK if you're "just looking"—"*Je regarde, merci.*"

Grand Department Stores: Paris invented the modern department store—different items under a single roof, with fixed prices—and several venerable places are still in business. The Galeries Lafayette flagship store, near the Opéra Garnier, features a sensational belle époque dome, a rooftop viewpoint, and fashion shows every Friday at 15:00 from March through November (40 Boulevard Haussman, www.galerieslafayette.com, reserve fashion show at tel. 01 42 82 30 25). A block west is Printemps, with cheaper prices and a better rooftop view.

Place de la Madeleine Neighborhood (Mo: Madeleine; ✪ see map on page 160): This ritzy area forms a miracle mile of gourmet food shops, glittering jewelry stores, five-star hotels, exclusive clothing boutiques, and people who spend more on clothes in a day than I do in a year. Stroll counterclockwise around Place de la Madeleine, with its Roman-temple-esque church. Start with the bastion of gourmet food stores, Fauchon. Peruse the deli and bakery, then cross the street to Fauchon's other outlet, and stroll downstairs to the wine cellar to consider a €5,000 bottle of Cognac.

Continuing around the square, don't miss Fauchon's rival, Hédiard (founded 1854), whose small red containers are popular souvenirs. At La Maison des Truffe, smell those truffles and ponder how something so ugly can cost €3,000 a pound. Continue past a tea store and a caviar store—fish eggs can sell for up to €12,000 a kilo.

To extend this walk, stroll down Rue Royale and turn left on Rue St. Honoré, then left again on Rue de Castiglione. End the walk on the *très* elegant square, Place Vendôme, home to upper-crust jewelry stores and the Hôtel Ritz.

Sèvres-Babylone to St. Sulpice (Mo: Sèvres-Babylone; ✪ see map on page 156): For Left Bank swank, start at the Bon Marché department store, Paris' oldest. Walk down Rue de Sèvres, and consider a drink at the terribly cool Au Savignon Café (#10). Continue on to the half-man-half-horse statue (ouch)—you're at a pinwheel intersection of several boutique-lined streets worth exploring. When you're ready, turn right on Rue du Vieux Colombier and head to St. Sulpice Church. To finish the walk, continue past the church on Rue St. Sulpice and turn left on Rue de Seine, to find Gérard Mulot's *pâtisserie* (#76) with arguably Paris' best pastries.

Flea Markets: The mother of all flea markets is the Puces St. Ouen, on Paris' northern fringe. More than 2,000 vendors in covered alleys sell everything from flamingos to faucets, but mostly antiques. It runs Saturday 9:00-18:00, Sunday 10:00-18:00, and Monday 11:00-17:00. From the Porte de Clignancourt Métro station, walk straight out of the station and pass under the freeway overpass. Veer left on Rue des Rosiers—the main "spine" of the sprawling market—and explore from there. No event brings together the melting-pot population of Paris better than this carnival-like market. Some find it claustrophobic, overcrowded, and threatening; others find French *diamants*-in-the-rough and return happy. For a smaller, less-touristed flea market, try the Puces de Vanves (Sat-Sun only, 7:00-17:00, Mo: Porte de Vanves).

Traffic-Free Shopping and Café Streets: Several traffic-free and generally open-air markets overflow with flowers, produce, fish vendors, and butchers, illustrating how most Parisians shopped before there were supermarkets and department stores. Shops are open daily except Sunday afternoons, Monday, and lunchtime (13:00 to 15:00 or 16:00).

Rue Cler is refined and upscale (Mo: Ecole Militaire, ✪ see the Rue Cler Walk, page 111). Rue Montorgueil, 10 blocks from the Louvre, has a more local scene with cafés and cute bistros (Mo: Etienne Marcel). Forum des Halles is a modern shopping mall under a striking glass-and-steel canopy (Mo: Les Halles). Rue Mouffetard, hiding several blocks behind the Panthéon, starts on picturesque Place Contrescarpe and becomes more Parisian the farther downhill you go (Mo: Censier Daubenton). In the heart of the Left Bank, try Rue de Seine and Rue de Buci (Mo: Odéon).

Souvenirs: You won't need a guidebook to find plenty of shops selling "I Heart Paris" T-shirts, *Mona Lisa* magnets, and Eiffel Tower keychains—especially along Rue de Rivoli (near the Louvre) and Rue d'Arcole (north of Notre-Dame). The riverfront stalls near Notre-Dame are classy and picturesque, if higher-priced.

Getting a VAT Refund: If you purchase more than €175 worth of goods at a single store, you may be eligible to get a refund of the 20 percent Value-Added Tax (VAT). Have the store fill out the paperwork, then, at the airport, get it stamped by Customs and processed by a VAT refund company. At Charles de Gaulle, you'll find them at the check-in area, or ask for help at an orange ADP info desk. Get more details from your merchant or see www.ricksteves.com/vat.

Customs for American Shoppers: You are allowed to take home $800 worth of items per person duty-free, once every 31 days. You can also bring in one liter of alcohol duty-free. As for food, you can take home many processed and packaged foods (e.g., vacuum-packed cheeses, chocolate, mustard) but no fresh produce or meats (canned pâtés are an exception). Any liquid-containing foods must be packed in checked luggage, a potential recipe for disaster. To check customs rules and duty rates, visit http://help.cbp.gov.

Nightlife

Paris is brilliant after dark. Perhaps the best after-dark activity is to enjoy a leisurely meal, then stroll historic streets, past floodlit squares and fountains.

Consulting the weekly *L'Officiel des Spectacles* (€1, comes out on Wed, www.offi.fr) is useful if you want to know what's going on in Paris. For help deciphering the all-French listings, see www.colleensparis.com.

Jazz and Blues Clubs: Paris has been a jazz capital since the Roaring 20s. At most clubs, expect to pay (about) a €20 entry plus €7 per drink. Caveau de la Huchette, in the Latin Quarter near Notre-Dame, is a steamy cellar for hot jazz and frenzied swing dancing (5 Rue de la Huchette, tel. 01 43 26 65 05, www.caveaudelahuchette.fr). Rue des Lombards, a street in central Paris (Mo: Châtelet), is a teeming two-block-long hive of nightlife. The plush Au Duc des Lombards club offers high-class jazz in a theater-like setting (42 Rue des Lombards, tel. 01 42 33 22 88, www.ducdeslombards. fr). Le Sunside, just a block away, has two different stages (60 Rue des Lombards, tel. 01 40 26 46 60, www.sunset-sunside.com).

Classical Concerts: Several historic churches regularly host concerts (mostly Baroque-style chamber music) from March through November: Sainte-Chapelle, St. Sulpice, St. Germain-des-Prés, La Madeleine, St. Eustache, and St. Julien-le-Pauvre. Sainte-Chapelle is especially worthwhile for the pleasure of hearing Mozart, Bach, or Vivaldi, surrounded by the stained glass of the tiny church (it's unheated—bring a sweater). Buy tickets there or make reservations (tel. 01 42 77 65 65 or 06 67 30 65 65, www.euromusicproductions.fr).

Opera is performed at the massive modern opera house, the Opéra Bastille (Mo: Bastille). The Opéra Garnier, Paris' first opera house, hosts opera and ballet in a grand belle époque setting (Mo: Opéra). Get tickets for either opera house at tel. 08 92 89 90 90, www.operadeparis.fr, or at their box offices.

Movies: Many theaters run movies in their original language (look for *"v.o."—version originale*). Cinemas cluster around Mo: Odéon. Enjoy the big movie palaces on the Champs-Elysées. Or, take in a movie at the Open Air Cinema at La Villette (Cinéma en Plein Air), your chance to relax on the grass and see a movie under the stars with happy Parisians (free, mid-July-Aug Wed-Sun, films start at dusk).

Rowdy Bars and Clubs: For late-night partying (after 21:00), try the Rue de Lappe—take the Métro to Bastille, head north and follow the noise. Other areas are around Rue Vieille du Temple in the Marais (Mo: St. Paul) and Rue des Canettes and Guisarde (Mo: St. Sulpice).

Museums: To check which museums have later opening hours on different evenings, ✪ see the "Paris at a Glance" sidebar on page 10.

Tours by Night: Consider a Seine River cruise or bus tour. Two companies that take up to three people on informal, fun, off-beat tours in old Deux Chevaux cars are Paris Authentic (mobile 06 64 50 44 19, www.parisauthentic.com) and 4 Roues Sous 1 Parapluie (mobile 06 67 32 26 68, www.4roues-sous-1parapluie.com). Do-it-yourselfers could snag a taxi or Uber and make their own scenic tour—from Notre-Dame to the Eiffel Tower along the Left Bank, then returning along the Right Bank (figure about €50 for a one-hour loop by taxi, €40 by Uber, split by up to four passengers).

Night Scenes: The Eiffel Tower viewed from Place du Trocadéro is spectacular, and the Trocadéro itself is a festival of hawkers, gawkers, drummers, and entertainers. The Champs-Elysées and Arc de Triomphe glitter after dark. Ile St. Louis (Mo: Pont Marie) is quiet and romantic; perfect for dinner, for sampling Paris' best ice cream shops, and for a stroll to floodlit Notre-Dame.

Get your Left Bank buzz in the area around Place St. Germain-des-Prés and Odéon (Mo: St. Germain-des-Prés and Odéon), full of famous cafés, cinemas, and night owls prowling along Rue des Canettes, Rue Guisarde, and Rue de Buci. Montmartre is touristy but lively, and a bit dicey at night. For old-time cabaret ambience, consider Au Lapin Agile (€28, shows in French only, tel. 01 46 06 85 87, www.au-lapin-agile.com), and end the evening in front of Sacré-Cœur Basilica for the glorious city view.

Connecting with the Culture

Make your trip more personal through one-on-one contact with real live English-speaking Parisians. A group called Meeting the French puts travelers in touch with locals who offer conversation groups, specialty tours, and more (www.meetingthefrench.com). Paris Greeter's volunteers guide you through "their" Paris (www.greeters.paris). Ô Château offers fun,

Those Parisians

The idea that Parisians are "mean and cold and refuse to speak English" is an out-of-date preconception left over from the days of Charles de Gaulle. Parisians are as friendly as any other people, and no more disagreeable than New Yorkers.

Parisians may appear cold when they're actually being polite and formal, respecting the fine points of culture and tradition. (From their view, those ever-smiling Americans, while friendly, are somewhat insincere.) And let's face it: It's tough to keep on smiling when you've been crushed by a Big Mac, Mickey Moused by Disney, and drowned in instant coffee.

Like many big cities, Paris is a massive melting pot of people from all over France plus recent immigrants. Your evening hotel receptionist may speak French with an accent.

To appreciate the French—slow down. Observe the French pace of life. Despite its size and modernity, Paris maintains a genuine village feel. People still hold the door open for you in the Métro. People share family news with their neighborhood grocer. And on warm summer nights, the streets and cafés are full of happy Parisians in love with life.

informal wine-tasting classes (www.o-chateau.com). Cooking schools have pricey demonstration courses—the most famous is Le Cordon Bleu (www.lcbparis.com). Parler Parlor lets you practice conversational French in a relaxed environment (www.parlerparlor.com). Or check out the people-to-people events at www.meetup.com.

Tours

Seine Cruises: Several companies run one-hour, €13-15 boat cruises on the Seine, best by night, and worth checking out for their dinner cruises. Bateaux-Mouches has large, open-topped, often-crowded boats departing from the Pont de l'Alma (www.bateaux-mouches.fr). Others are Bateaux Parisiens (from the Eiffel Tower, www.bateauxparisiens.com) and Vedettes du Pont Neuf (from Pont Neuf, www.vedettesdupontneuf.com). Batobus allows you to get on and off, making their day passes worthwhile for point-A-to-B travel (www.batobus.com).

Bus Tours: Hop-on, hop-off bus tours let you ride through Paris on an open-air bus. Hop on at any of the stops along their loop routes, pay as you board (€33 for a day), ride awhile, hop off to sightsee, then catch the next one to carry on. Of the various companies, L'OpenTour is best (www.paris.opentour.com). City Vision offers uninspired bus tours for tricky-to-reach excursions outside the city, e.g., to D-Day beaches or the Loire (www.pariscityvision.com).

Guided Tours: For walking tours of Paris' history, art, and neighborhoods, try Paris Walks (www.paris-walks.com). Context Travel is serious and intellectual (www.contexttravel.com). Fat Tire Tours' Classic Paris Walking Tour is the antithesis—low-brow and high-fun, while their "Skip the Line" tours of major sights can be worthwhile at Sainte-Chapelle, the Eiffel Tower—if you weren't able to reserve ahead, and Notre-Dame Tower (www.fattiretours.com/paris).

Bike tours guide a dozen cyclists on breezy excursions through neighborhoods. Try Bike About Tours, near Notre-Dame (www.bikeabout-tours.com) or Fat Tire Bike Tours, near the Eiffel Tower (www.fattiretours.com/paris).

If you'd like a private guide (around €200/half-day), try Arnaud Servignat (tel. 06 68 80 29 05, www.french-guide.com), Thierry Gauduchon (tel. 06 19 07 30 77, tgauduchon@gmail.com), or Elizabeth Van Hest (tel. 01 43 41 47 31, elisa.guide@gmail.com).

RESOURCES FROM RICK STEVES

This Pocket guide is one of dozens of titles in my series of guidebooks on European travel. I also produce a public television series, *Rick Steves' Europe,* and a public radio show, *Travel with Rick Steves.* My website, www.ricksteves.com, offers a wealth of free travel information, including videos and podcasts of my shows and classes, audio tours of Europe's great sights, travel forums, guidebook updates, my travel blog, and my guide to European rail passes—plus an online travel store and information on our tours of Europe.

How Was Your Trip? You can share your tips, concerns, and discoveries at www.ricksteves.com/feedback. I value your feedback. Thanks in advance.

French Survival Phrases

When using the phonetics, try to nasalize the n̲ sound.

English	French	Phonetics
Good day.	Bonjour.	bohn-zhoor
Mrs. / Mr.	Madame / Monsieur	mah-dahm / muhs-yur
Do you speak English?	Parlez-vous anglais?	par-lay-voo ahn-glay
Yes. / No.	Oui. / Non.	wee / nohn
I understand.	Je comprends.	zhuh kohn-prahn
I don't understand.	Je ne comprends pas.	zhuh nuh kohn-prahn pah
Please.	S'il vous plaît.	see voo play
Thank you.	Merci.	mehr-see
I'm sorry.	Désolé.	day-zoh-lay
Excuse me.	Pardon.	par-dohn
(No) problem.	(Pas de) problème.	(pah duh) proh-blehm
It's good.	C'est bon.	say bohn
Goodbye.	Au revoir.	oh vwahr
one / two	un / deux	uhn / duh
three / four	trois / quatre	twah / kah-truh
five / six	cinq / six	sank / sees
seven / eight	sept / huit	seht / weet
nine / ten	neuf / dix	nuhf / dees
How much is it?	Combien?	kohn-bee-an
Write it?	Ecrivez?	ay-kree-vay
Is it free?	C'est gratuit?	say grah-twee
Included?	Inclus?	an-klew
Where can I buy / find...?	Où puis-je acheter / trouver...?	oo pwee-zhuh ah-shuh-tay / troo-vay
I'd like / We'd like...	Je voudrais / Nous voudrions...	zhuh voo-dray / noo voo-dree-ohn
...a room.	...une chambre.	ewn shahn-bruh
...a ticket to ___.	...un billet pour ___.	uhn bee-yay poor
Is it possible?	C'est possible?	say poh-see-bluh
Where is...?	Où est...?	oo ay
...the train station	...la gare	lah gar
...the bus station	...la gare routière	lah gar root-yehr
...tourist information	...l'office du tourisme	loh-fees dew too-reez-muh
Where are the toilets?	Où sont les toilettes?	oo sohn lay twah-leht
men	hommes	ohm
women	dames	dahm
left / right	à gauche / à droite	ah gohsh / ah dwaht
straight	tout droit	too dwah
When does this open / close?	Ça ouvre / ferme à quelle heure?	sah oo-vruh / fehrm ah kehl ur
At what time?	À quelle heure?	ah kehl ur
Just a moment.	Un moment.	uhn moh-mahn
now / soon / later	maintenant / bientôt / plus tard	man-tuh-nahn / bee-an-toh / plew tar
today / tomorrow	aujourd'hui / demain	oh-zhoor-dwee / duh-man

Practicalities

In the Restaurant

English	French	Pronunciation
I'd like / We'd like...	**Je voudrais / Nous voudrions...**	zhuh voo-dray / noo voo-dree-ohn
...to reserve...	**...réserver...**	ray-zehr-vay
...a table for one / two.	**...une table pour un / deux.**	ewn tah-bluh poor uhn / duh
Non-smoking.	**Non fumeur.**	nohn few-mur
Is this seat free?	**C'est libre?**	say lee-bruh
The menu (in English), please.	**La carte (en anglais), s'il vous plaît.**	lah kart (ahn ahn-glay) see voo play
service (not) included	**service (non) compris**	sehr-vees (nohn) kohn-pree
to go	**à emporter**	ah ahn-por-tay
with / without	**avec / sans**	ah-vehk / sahn
and / or	**et / ou**	ay / oo
special of the day	**plat du jour**	plah dew zhoor
specialty of the house	**spécialité de la maison**	spay-see-ah-lee-tay duh lah may-zohn
appetizers	**hors-d'oeuvre**	or-duh-vruh
first course (soup, salad)	**entrée**	ahn-tray
main course (meat, fish)	**plat principal**	plah pran-see-pahl
bread	**pain**	pan
cheese	**fromage**	froh-mahzh
sandwich	**sandwich**	sahnd-weech
soup	**soupe**	soop
salad	**salade**	sah-lahd
meat	**viande**	vee-ahnd
chicken	**poulet**	poo-lay
fish	**poisson**	pwah-sohn
seafood	**fruits de mer**	frwee duh mehr
mineral water	**eau minérale**	oh mee-nay-rahl
tap water	**l'eau du robinet**	loh dew roh-bee-nay
milk	**lait**	lay
(orange) juice	**jus (d'orange)**	zhew (doh-rahnzh)
coffee	**café**	kah-fay
tea	**thé**	tay
wine	**vin**	van
red / white	**rouge / blanc**	roozh / blahn
glass / bottle	**verre / bouteille**	vehr / boo-teh-ee
beer	**bière**	bee-ehr
Cheers!	**Santé!**	sahn-tay
More. / Another.	**Plus. / Un autre.**	plew / uhn oh-truh
The same.	**La même chose.**	lah mehm shohz
The bill, please.	**L'addition, s'il vous plaît.**	lah-dee-see-ohn see voo play
tip	**pourboire**	poor-bwar
Delicious!	**Délicieux!**	day-lee-see-uh

For more user-friendly French phrases, check out *Rick Steves' French Phrase Book and Dictionary* or *Rick Steves' French, Italian & German Phrase Book*.

INDEX

PHOTO CREDITS

Photo Credits continued on next page

Practicalities
p. 196 © Ritu Jethani/123rf.com

Start your trip at

Our website enhances this book and turns

Explore Europe

At ricksteves.com you can browse through thousands of articles, videos, photos and radio interviews, plus find a wealth of money-saving travel tips for planning your dream trip. And with our mobile-friendly website, you can easily access all this great travel information anywhere you go.

TV Shows

Preview the places you'll visit by watching entire half-hour episodes of Rick Steves' Europe (choose from all 100 shows) on-demand, for free.

ricksteves.com

your travel dreams into affordable reality

Radio Interviews

Enjoy ready access to Rick's vast library of radio interviews covering

travel tips and cultural insights that relate specifically to your Europe travel plans.

Travel Forums

Learn, ask, share! Our online community of savvy travelers is a great resource for first-time travelers to Europe, as well as seasoned pros. You'll find forums on each country, plus travel tips and restaurant/hotel reviews. You can even ask one of our well-traveled staff to chime in with an opinion.

Travel News

Subscribe to our free Travel News e-newsletter, and get monthly updates from Rick on what's happening in Europe.

Audio Europe™

Rick's Free Travel App

Get your FREE Rick Steves Audio Europe™ app to enjoy...

- Dozens of self-guided tours of Europe's top museums, sights and historic walks
- Hundreds of tracks filled with cultural insights and sightseeing tips from Rick's radio interviews
- All organized into handy geographic playlists
- For Apple and Android

With Rick whispering in your ear, Europe gets even better.

Find out more at ricksteves.com

Pack Light and Right

Rick Steves has

Experience maximum Europe

Save time and energy

This guidebook is your independent-travel toolkit. But for all it delivers, it's still up to you to devote the time and energy it takes to manage the preparation and logistics that are essential for a happy trip. If that's a hassle, there's a solution.

Rick Steves Tours

A Rick Steves tour takes you to Europe's most interesting places with great guides and small groups

great tours, too!

with minimum stress

of 28 or less. We follow Rick's favorite itineraries, ride in comfy buses, stay in family-run hotels, and bring you intimately close to the Europe you've traveled so far to see. Most importantly, we take away the logistical headaches so you can focus on the fun.

of them repeat customers—along with us on four dozen different itineraries, from Ireland to Italy to Istanbul. Is a Rick Steves tour the right fit for your travel dreams? Find out at ricksteves.com, where you can also request Rick's latest tour catalog.

Join the fun
This year we'll take thousands of free-spirited travelers—nearly half

Europe is best experienced with happy travel partners. We hope you can join us.

See our itineraries at ricksteves.com

A Guide for Every Trip

BEST OF GUIDES

Full color easy-to-scan format, focusing on Europe's most popular destinations and sights.

Best of England
Best of Europe
Best of France
Best of Germany
Best of Ireland
Best of Italy
Best of Spain

COMPREHENSIVE GUIDES

City, country, and regional guides with detailed coverage for a multi-week trip exploring iconic sights and more.

Amsterdam & the Netherlands
Barcelona
Belgium: Bruges, Brussels,
  Antwerp & Ghent
Berlin
Budapest
Croatia & Slovenia

Eastern Europe
England
Florence & Tuscany
France
Germany
Great Britain
Greece: Athens
  & the Peloponnese
Iceland
Ireland
Istanbul
Italy
London
Paris
Portugal
Prague & the Czech Republic
Provence & the French Riviera
Rome
Scandinavia
Scotland
Spain
Switzerland
Venice
Vienna, Salzburg & Tirol

Rick Steves guidebooks are published by Avalon Travel,
an imprint of Perseus Books, a Hachette Book Group company.

POCKET GUIDES

Amsterdam
Athens
Barcelona
Florence
Italy's Cinque Terre
London

Munich & Salzburg
Paris
Prague
Rome
Venice
Vienna

SNAPSHOT GUIDES

Focused single-destination coverage.

Basque Country: Spain & France
Copenhagen & the Best of Denmark
Dublin
Dubrovnik
Edinburgh
Hill Towns of Central Italy
Krakow, Warsaw & Gdansk
Lisbon
Loire Valley
Madrid & Toledo
Milan & the Italian Lakes District
Naples & the Amalfi Coast
Northern Ireland
Normandy
Norway
Reykjavik
Sevilla, Granada & Southern Spain
St. Petersburg, Helsinki & Tallinn
Stockholm

CRUISE PORTS GUIDES

Reference for cruise ports of call.

Mediterranean Cruise Ports
Scandinavian & Northern European
  Cruise Ports

TRAVEL SKILLS & CULTURE

Europe 101
European Christmas
European Easter
European Festivals
Europe Through the Back Door
Postcards from Europe
Travel as a Political Act

PHRASE BOOKS & DICTIONARIES

French
French, Italian & German
German
Italian
Portuguese
Spanish

PLANNING MAPS

Britain, Ireland & London
Europe
France & Paris
Germany, Austria & Switzerland
Ireland
Italy
Spain & Portugal

Avalon Travel
An imprint of Perseus Books
A Hachette Book Group company
1700 Fourth Street
Berkeley, CA 94710

Printed in China by RR Donnelley
Third Edition
Third printing October 2018

ISBN 978-1-63121-563-6
ISSN 2158-8503

For the latest on Rick's lectures, guidebooks, tours, public radio show, and public
television series, contact Rick Steves' Europe, 130 Fourth Avenue North, Edmonds,
WA 98020, tel. 425/771-8303, fax 425/771-0833, ricksteves.com, or rick@ricksteves.
com.

Rick Steves' Europe
Managing Editor: Jennifer Madison Davis
Special Publications Manager: Risa Laib
Editors: Glenn Eriksen, Tom Griffin, Katherine Gustafson, Suzanne Kotz, Cathy Lu,
John Pierce, Carrie Shepherd
Editorial & Production Assistant: Jessica Shaw
Researcher: Mary Bouron, Virginie Moré
Graphic Content Director: Sandra Hundacker
Maps & Graphics: David C. Hoerlein, Lauren Mills, Mary Rostad

Avalon Travel
Senior Editor and Series Manager: Madhu Prasher
Editor: Jamie Andrade
Associate Editor: Sierra Machado
Copy Editor: Maggie Ryan
Proofreader: Jamie Leigh Real
Indexer: Stephen Callahan
Production & Typesetting: Christine DeLorenzo
Cover Design: Kimberly Glyder Design
Interior Design: Darren Alessi
Maps & Graphics: Kat Bennett, Mike Morgenfeld, Brice Ticen
Front Cover Image: © S. Greg Panosian/Getty Images

ABOUT THE AUTHORS

Rick Steves

Since 1973, Rick has spent about four months a year exploring Europe. His mission: to empower Americans to have European trips that are fun, affordable, and culturally broadening. Rick produces a best-selling guidebook series, a public television series, and a public radio show, and organizes small-group tours that take over 20,000 travelers to Europe annually. He does all of this with the help of a hardworking, well-traveled staff of 100 at Rick Steves' Europe in Edmonds, Washington, near Seattle. When not on the road, Rick is active in his church and with advocacy groups focused on economic justice, drug policy reform, and ending hunger. To recharge, Rick plays piano, relaxes at his family cabin in the Cascade Mountains, and spends time with his partner Trish, son Andy, and daughter Jackie. Find out more about Rick at www.ricksteves.com and on Facebook.

Steve Smith

Steve Smith manages tour guides for Rick Steves' Europe tour programs and has been researching guidebooks with Rick for over two decades. Fluent in French, he's lived in France on several occasions, starting when he was seven. Steve owns a restored farmhouse in rural Burgundy where he hangs his beret in research season. Steve's wife, Karen Lewis Smith—an expert on French cuisine and wine— provides invaluable contributions to his books.

Gene Openshaw

Gene has co-authored a dozen Rick Steves books, specializing in writing walks and tours of Europe's cities, museums, and cultural sights. He also contributes to Rick's public television series, produces tours for Rick Steves Audio Europe, and is a regular guest on Rick's public radio show. Outside of the travel world, Gene has co-authored *The Seattle Joke Book*. As a composer, Gene has written a full-length opera called *Matter* (soundtrack available on Amazon), a violin sonata, and dozens of songs. He lives near Seattle with his daughter, enjoys giving presentations on art and history, and roots for the Mariners in good times and bad.

FOLDOUT COLOR MAP

The foldout map on the opposite page includes:
- A map of Paris on one side
- Maps of Greater Paris, Montemarte, Historic Paris Walk, Day Trips, and Paris Métro on the other side